A Cry for
HELP

Who's Listening?

Carletha Brown

A CRY FOR HELP: WHO'S LISTENING?

This book is written to provide information and motivation to readers. Its purpose is not to render any type of psychological, legal, or professional advice of any kind. The content is the sole opinion and expression of the author, and not necessarily that of the publisher.

Copyright © 2019 by Carletha Brown

All rights reserved. No part of this book may be reproduced, transmitted, or distributed in any form by any means, including, but not limited to, recording, photocopying, or taking screenshots of parts of the book, without prior written permission from the author or the publisher. Brief quotations for noncommercial purposes, such as book reviews, permitted by Fair Use of the U.S. Copyright Law, are allowed without written permissions, as long as such quotations do not cause damage to the book's commercial value. For permissions, write to the publisher, whose address is stated below.

Printed in the United States of America.

ISBN   978-1-64552-011-5   (Paperback)
ISBN   978-1-64552-012-2   (Digital)

Lettra Press books may be ordered through booksellers or by contacting:

Lettra Press LLC
18229 E 52nd Ave.
Denver City, CO 80249
1 303 586 1431 | info@lettrapress.com
www.lettrapress.com

Contents

Acknowledgement vii
Introduction ix

Chapter 1: 1
Chapter 2: Off To New York 4
Chapter 3: Back To Hell 6
Chapter 4: The First Time 14
Chapter 5: Another Gift From God 23
Chapter 6: Tortured 29
Chapter 7: First Husband 39
Chapter 8: New City For Me 58
Chapter 9: Husband # Two 67
Chapter 10: A Change Is Coming 76
Chapter 11: Preacher Man 86
Chapter 12: Nobody But God 122

Acknowledgement

First, I would like to thank my two daughters. Angela Herbert and Levoia Thompson for being born into my life, because even though I made a lot of mistakes, you continued to be there for me when I needed you most.

I would like to thank my eight grandchildren—Dyneshia, Samantha, Bernard, Gerald, Paul, Steve, Carletha, and Oswald, who really kept their grandmother laughing and worried, for understanding that sometimes I treated you as if I was your mother it was all for the sake of love.

I would like to thank my son-in-law, Darryl Herbert for loving my daughter and for accepting my five grandchildren as your own. When I asked you the day of your wedding to please always love my daughter and not hurt her, you told me you will always be there for her and her children. You are still here fifteen years later. You both are very blessed to have each other. And I thank you for never telling me no. Than you for caring for me.

I would love to thank my sisters Elouise Williams and Louise Williams for having patience with a big sister that was always worried about you both and trying to protect you. I would like to thank Elouise for helping me with this book and taking good care of me when I was so sick, your love and kindness will never be forgotten. We suffered a great loss, and that was your twin, Louise Williams. She lost her battle to breast cancer five years ago, 2009.

I would like to thank my sister Laura Morgan for all the phone calls to check on me and for keeping me encouraged when I see you I see strength and courage. Thanks for your love and support.

I would love to thank my second mom, Mz. Betty Joe Hill, for always being there for me, thank you for your support, for being a loyal customer and for all your phone calls. Love you very much. Thank you for helping me remain calm and reminding me to always pray.

I would like to thank Mr. Woodbury for all your moral support, thank you for the fruits and keeping me focus on what God can do. You always listen to my heartaches and complaints and never judge me. You always say "you're on a winning team!! God Bless you and your family, you are truly a friend to the very end.

I would like to thank Mrs. Mary Evans for always believing in me when I didn't believe in myself, for pushing me to dream the impossible. Thank you for all of your financial and moral support. You never gave up on me, you have always been someone I looked up to, and I was always amazed at watching your courage and strength.

I would like to thank Ms. Rebecca Mapp for always being a true friend and customer. You opened your door for me when I needed you most. Thanks for the visits from you and your father and for the flowers. You have never said no to me no matter how busy your schedule was for you. I commend you. Love you always.

I want to thank Pearlie Hill, Betty Joe Hill, Rebecca Mapp, Cynthia Stewart, Pamela Moreland, Carolyn Mack, Ms. McFadden, and Mary Evans for always trusting me to take care of your hair for more than Twenty Years! Sorry, I'm no longer able to, I miss you all very much. Thanks for all of your support and advice throughout the years. LOVE TO YOU ALL ALWAYS AND FOREVER!

Introduction

My name is Carletha Brown, Burton, Lavender, Lovely. Married and divorced three times. With each divorce I asked for my maiden name back. I am a mother of two daughters and eight adult grandchildren, and three great grandchildren. I'm taking this time out in my life to write my story because there are so many children and adults crying out for help. They cannot afford a Dr. Phil or Oprah or trust anyone enough to talk to them. At one point of time I tried to reach out to both Dr. Phil and Oprah and hit a dead end each time. I've always wondered how people get in touch with them. Twenty-five or more years prior, I began writing Oprah a letter when she had Erica Kane on her show, and the All My Children husbands. The letter turned into a book!! I never tried to send it. I called it WILL THE REAL ERICA KANE PLEASE STAND UP. (All the men I loved.) Not who loved me, because I really can't tell who loved me. My journey took me to hell and back and through all my trials and tribulation, I had to come back to Jesus. When He said I will never leave nor forsake you, He meant just that. It gets hard sometimes to believe it, but when you keep hitting a brick wall and facing death so many times you start wondering, "Why am I still here?" It's not as though we can stand in a line and pick our race or our mother and father. "Wow! Would life be any different?" Believe me, it's only by the grace of God that any of us are still here. We all have a purpose for being on this earth. My belief and my purpose is to encourage others to believe in yourself and trust that God really does have your back no matter what the devil throws your way. As the song say, "He Paid It All." (Meaning) Jesus paid for our sins, and I thank Him for allowing me to be alive long enough to acknowledge that. This is my story:

Chapter 1

I was born in Belle Glade FL. My mother was a very strong woman. I could remember her working in the celery fields almost every day. I had four brothers and one sister by my mom. I remember when I was five, my dad came and stole me and my younger brother and took us to Ft Pierce, FL, to his home. My mother was working that day. She had no clue he was coming. I always wondered about the look on her face or her reaction when she found us gone. The home that my father took us to, was his, his new wife and her five daughters. They were all total strangers to me, including him. All I knew is that he said he was our daddy. It was so much abuse in that home. My father abusing their mother and the oldest daughter was abusing me physically and mentally. She would always wait until late at night when we were supposed to be asleep to do her damage to me. My dad made me call their mother, mom and they had to call him daddy. The oldest daughter would fight and scratch my face and say, that is not your momma!!! And I would try to fight back and say, that is not your daddy. My dad use to accuse their mom of cheating and he would hit her in front of us. It had us very afraid of him and we would scream and cry for him to stop, but it didn't help. I can remember that good ole welfare cheese and canned meat. We had to eat out of pot lids and drink out of peanut butter and mayonnaise jars. I cried for my mom every night. I didn't understand why I never saw my mom anymore. I remember my dad would always beat me and my brother with a palmetto stick. Sometimes we had to go pick it off the tree for our own beatings. According to his mood he would either leave the stickers on it or slice them off. When they would say," I want to see blood"!!!! they would leave them on. Sometimes my brother's punishment was my dad putting him in the trunk of his car. The very first time as I remember, he was in there almost all night. We would cry for him and I would beg my dad to let him out. Sometimes my tears would work and sometimes it wouldn't. I always tried to protect my brother from my dad. Also, there was one sister that I tried to protect because she got the most beatings out of all the siblings. Sometimes her punishment was to be put in a dark closet or tied to a chair in sitting position while she was being beaten. I promised her that I would always come back and rescue her, no matter what. I got use to the beatings. It's just that no matter what you did or didn't do, you got a beating from somewhere in that house. I remember my dad telling me that he was a preacher. Ha! Not in a church, in the back yard with a loud bull horn. I was so upset with him. He had me going door to door selling family Bibles. He taught me what to say and how to say it. He tried to teach me how not to get turned away. If I got turned away that was a beating. I hated it!!!!! It was totally embarrassing going to those people house. Sometimes when people tried to tell me no, I would beg them to please listen to me. My dad would sit out in the car and wait on me to come out. Oh yes, he was the one taking me in different areas to go door to door. After that died down, he was a root man. He started having snakes and frogs etc… in the house. He and his best friend use to pretend they were healers and removing spells off people. I remember early one morning I could hear him and my stepmom whispering saying I hope she don't move. So just in case it was me, I didn't move. One of his deadly coral snakes had got out of the jar. (I wonder how, if they were in a jar?). The snake was in the bed crawling. Yes, it was me. My dad removed the snake and I got up out of bed. Things got so bad with them fighting. They decided to get a divorce. By then she had birth two sons from my father. I do remember my dad cheating with other women when he was married to her. He would always take me to different women houses and dare me to say anything. We moved out and my dad rented an apartment for me him and my brother. It hurt so bad, because now I was leaving a sister that I promised I would protect. But I also promise her that I would return when I got old enough to get her. I cried for me and her.

Chapter 2

OFF TO NEW YORK

My dad had an Aunt that lived in Utica, NY. She wanted me to come stay with her. One of my stepsisters that I didn't want to go went also to NY to live with my Aunt. That's when I was introduced to church and knowing God. I was around nine or ten years old. My Aunt was a true Christian woman. She lived two steps down from the church. After about two months of me fighting my stepsister and verbally abusing her she wanted to go back home. Why not, that's what I learned at home. My aunt sent her back to her mother, and I remain in NY. I loved when she left because she was the main reason my favorite sister was being abuse. To me, she is and always have been her mom's favorite child. But by me being so young I forgot that when she returned home all the beatings would start again for my favorite sister. We were so close because we got the most beatings and we never understood why. I would sneak and hold her and cry with her most of the time when I was living with them. I thank God for sending me there with my aunt because that's where I learned how to sing and most of all (Pray). Never knowing during this lifetime, I would need to PRAY. My Aunt use to make me get up and sing PASS ME NOT O GENTLE SAVIOUR. Every time it was time for me to sing, that was the only song I sang. Never knew why until my adult life. Still at times I didn't realize the magnitude of the song until now. I was so happy there with her until she would send me to her son's house to play with his daughter because my aunt's son used to rub his hands on me. I would look at him and run to his daughter and sit beside her. One day I was going upstairs to use the bathroom and when I looked, he was standing up there naked pulling on his self. I did not know the purpose of what he had in his hand, but I knew it didn't feel right. He was becking for me to come upstairs, but I wouldn't go. Later that night I was in the bed and he woke me up touching my leg under the cover. He was down on his knees and I started crying. His wife came and caught him and said to him, "Leave that little girl alone, if you want some p---sy come and get some grown lady p---y." Then he got up and left with her. Later that day I asked his wife to please take me home to my aunt house. After that, every time my aunt asked me if I wanted to go play with his daughter, I would say, "No ma'am." She never made me go, although she always thought I was lonely. I never told anyone what happen because his wife already knew, and she stopped him that time. But I don't know what would have happened the next time and I wasn't going to find out. I started eating a lot and gained a lot of weight because I thought it was something that I did. I became so afraid of him and his wife. My aunt was talking about sending me to learn how to ice skate and have those spots on my leg removed. For the summer she sent me to a convent school full of NUNS. I had a ball there. I even learn how to swim, and they taught me etiquette. They even created a Hawaiian play and I was one of the hula dancers. That was happy time for me. After about a year, she came and sat me down and said, "Your dad want you to come home." I scream and cried, "No!" She said it was nothing she could do but send me home. I prayed, but God wasn't listening to me anymore. My aunt was the nicest person I had ever met. There was no one that loved me the way she did. She said, he was crying and said he missed his daughter. He told her he keep playing this song, I'm waiting for my child to come home.

Chapter 3

BACK TO HELL

I came home to Ft. Pierce, FL. I came home to a man that had several women in his life. The first woman I met had a daughter the same age I was. She was a school teacher. Everything was fine for a while until early one morning my dad dropped me off to her house around 2:00 a.m. I remember her coming to the door to make sure I got in the house safe. Her daughter was in her bed. She said her daughter was sick. My dad left me there! This lady took me in her daughter's room and sat me on her bed, and then she sat beside me. She ask was I ok. I shook my head yes. Then she got up and I thought she was going to turn on the lights because the only light was coming from her bathroom. Instead she closed the door, and then sat back on the bed beside me.

I started sobbing. She said, "It's ok," in a soft voice. I couldn't see her it was so dark. She started rubbing my thighs and asked me if I had on any panties. By then I was crying like a baby. I said to her, I got to go to the bathroom! She opened the door and was asking me to be quiet. By then I was losing my mind crying. I was sitting on the toilet and heard her daughter calling for me.

She went inside where her daughter was to calm her down. While she was in there trying to calm her, I ran to the back door of her house trying to escape, but she had to have at least ten locks on that door. I ran to the front door and the same amount of locks was on that door.

I heard dogs barking outside. It sounded as if it was about 50 dogs out there, but I would have rather gotten eaten up by the dogs then to have this adult school teacher/mother sexually molest me. At that age, I didn't know the words for it. I just knew it didn't feel right. When she heard me trying to get out of the front door, she came to me and tried to stop me from unlocking the locks. Her daughter start yelling, "Carletha!!! What's wrong?" For whatever reason, my dad came back knocking while I was trying to get out. When she opened the door, I ran into my dad arms and I begged him to take me home. He asked her what was wrong with me, she said she is crying because my daughter is sick. My dad put me in the car and when we almost reached home, I told him what really happened. He slammed on breaks and said, "What?" I will go back there and kill that bitch. I begged him to keep driving and I never wanted to see her again. Well that didn't last long. He never left me alone with her again, but he didn't stop dating her. I guess he didn't believe me. She used to chase me around the yard as if she was playing with me. Every time she would catch up to me, she would rub on my chest or butt. I would be running for my life with fear written all over my face and she could care less. My dad would be in her house watching television. I was happy when that relationship ended. I heard she moved out of town.

Next thing I knew my brother is back with our dad after returning home to our mom and getting in a little trouble. My dad had his own plan for us. He had us picking tomatoes, cucumbers, oranges, grapefruits, lemons, limes, or whatever work there was that day. Believe me that was his money and he didn't play about his money. It started where we were only going on weekends. That was fun because a lot of kids went to the tomatoes field. Then it change to school days and any work that was going on that day. Sometimes the work bus would be loading up the same time as the school bus and the kids would make fun of us. I remember one day my brother and I went to pick some oranges and the trees was what we would call naked. My brother and I decided to walk home because we thought our dad would understand that the trees was practically bare. Sad mistake. My dad beat the both of us. He beat my brother with his fist and beat me with an extension cord. He would throw me in the air and on the way down see how quick he can hit me. After our beating, he took us back to the field and told us to pick what they had! We made 8 dollars all day, and he took that!!! My brother and I worked for him like little slaves. We would make sure that his money was right. Our dad never offered us any of our money that we worked hard for. We shed a lot of tears, just getting up in the mornings and other children are going to school while my brother and I was trying to figure out what work bus to jump on. The children use to laugh and pick on us about our dad. Our dad had built a tremendous amount of fear in us for him. We knew he didn't play about work, so we didn't either. Times got so bad for my brother and I, because now my dad only had us to beat on. When we did get a chance to go to school my brother had so much anger locked inside, he would take it out on the teachers. One day I came home from school and my brother's lips was so big they could cover the room. Soon as I walked in the house my dad told me what he did in school. My brother would look at me with those sad puppy eyes and shake his head without my dad looking at him. When my dad would leave the house, I would grab my brother and hold him and we would cry together. Another time my dad asked my brother to wash the dishes, but my brother didn't know my dad had fish rap up in newspaper on the table. He thought it was trash. My brother threw the paper in the garbage. When my dad came looking for the fish, he saw the newspaper in the garbage. He grabbed my brother up and punched him in the face, I start screaming, "No daddy!! Please daddy stop!" He then looked at me and told me I better not shed not one got damn tear. He had this look about him that you knew you better shut up. I sucked up my tears and said, "Who? I'm not crying." My brother looked at me so sad because he knew all hell had broken loose. My dad grabbed him and put him in the trunk of his car. I ran out behind him and I could hear him inside kicking and screaming. I jumped on top of the trunk and started crying and screaming for my dad to let him out. I didn't know time back then, but It seems like he was in there forever. My dad finally gave in and let him out. He took me in the house and made me strip to my panties and top and whipped me with a palmetto stick with stickers on it to draw blood, because I cried for my brother. We both were building hate towards him. Another time I remember my dad had got a call to come get my brother from school because he had body slammed a teacher. My dad was cursing at him as he walked up to my brother and hit him in the pit of his stomach. My brother fell to the floor and couldn't catch his breath. I fell to the floor beside him holding him trying to help him. I prayed and asked God to help him please. Suddenly, he started breathing. My dad didn't even care. I helped him up and took him to the bedroom, so he could try to sleep. The next person my dad met was a child like me. I didn't know at the time how old she was, but I knew she was young. She looked like a grown woman because she was big for her age. I think I was 12 my brother was 13 and she was 15 when we met her. She was crazy about my dad. He eventually moved her in with us. Wow! How they use to physically fight each other. She would fight my dad like a man, but he wore her down too. She started trying to boss me around as if she was my mother. One day we started arguing because she demanded me to do something. I said, "No! You're not my mother!!" At the time I was shooting darts at the dart board laughing at her. She called me a red bitch. I called her a black bitch. She charged at me and I started stabbing her in the chest with the dart. I stabbed her 4 or 5 times in her breast. When she saw blood, she backed away from me. I was so scared. I knew my dad was going to kill me. This time he took me and talked to me, but he was angry. He explained to me that I could give her breast cancer. I told him she hit me first. Another time I remember my brother and I got into a fight. I don't even remember why, I just remember it was bad. We had never fought each other. This was bad because we both had so much anger built inside of us. My dad's girlfriend was home. Thank God, because one of us may have died or seriously hurt each other. I know I was trying to. We were fighting so hard we had the couch standing straight up in the air. I looked on the table and grabbed the iron. As I was coming down with it to hit him in the head my dad's girlfriend grabbed it out of my hand and stopped us from fighting. I told my brother I was going to tell our dad when he gets home. My brother said to me, "I don't care if you tell daddy mammy." At that time, I ran to my ex stepmother's house which was about 5 miles from where we lived. I told her what happened. She told me to stay there until my dad comes to pick me up. About an hour or two later my dad came with my brother in the car with him. I can tell my dad was so mad with us. He asked me what happened and all I knew would make my dad even angrier at my brother than me was to tell him what he said about his momma. I said, "And I told him I was going to tell you, and he said, I don't care if you tell daddy mammy." My daddy was double mad then. My brother never saw my dad coming towards him. My dad was a security guard. He had this iron black jack in his back pocket. As he walked up to my brother, he took it out and started hitting my brother in his head with it, blood was shooting out like a faucet. I could hear my brother screaming and balling up covering his head. I ran to the car and grabbed my dad's hand and told him that I lied so he would stop hitting him. He slapped me down on the ground. I kept telling my brother how sorry I was. We made a bond that we would never fight each other ever again, and no matter what we would always have each other's back. I thank my dad's girlfriend for stopping me from hitting my brother with that iron. They stayed together for a while. One day it was myself, my brother and this young lady at the house. My brother was lying on the floor looking at tv and I was sitting on the couch. This young lady kept jumping across my brother's head as he lied on the floor. She had on a skirt and no panties. I started yelling at her telling her to leave my brother alone because I knew my dad would kill him. She wouldn't stop even my brother was asking her to leave him alone. She kept pulling her skirt over his head. Then she grabbed him up and pulled him to my dad's bedroom and pushed the door, but it didn't close all the way. He was having sex with her. As I watched them, I started screaming, "Daddy gonna kill yall!" I never said a word to my dad because I knew my dad would kill him. My brother begged my dad to please send him to our mom for a little while. He did. After that, the fights continued. This young girl had two more children from my daddy. I always wondered why her children's last name was the same as hers. Now I know. She was too young to tell anyone that those were his old behind children!!! One night before she had the children, I was sitting on my bed with a slip and a top on facing my bedroom window. I felt strange, as if someone was watching me. I laid down and fell asleep and I promise I know now that it was God that woke me up. There stood this big tall man standing over me saying, "Be quiet." I screamed, "Daddy!!: He said once again, "Be quiet." I jumped up in my bed and I saw his hands on his penis moving in and out. I ran out my room into my dad's room where he and her were asleep. I told him there was a man in my room. He jumped up in his underwear and the man ran out the back door from which he came, dropping white semen all over the floor. My dad ran after him in his underwear and he caught him. He called the police and they arrested the man. That night my dad swore that his young lady was seeing this man and he was looking for her. There was a soda top left in the window, so he said she left it there, so the man could come in for her. He beat the crap out of her that night. The next day at school everyone had heard about it. Some of the kids picked at me and said you know that was your daddy in your room! Then there was a rumor that I put an innocent man in jail. More tears.... She moved out.

One morning around 2 or 3am, my dad woke me up to scratch his back. I never had any fingernails, so my dad would give me a soda bottle top to use. I was so sleepy. He had this huge mold right on the top of his neck. I was scratching and going to sleep. I hit that mold hard with that top. I began telling him that I was sorry. He slapped me so hard that I flew across the room. I told him that I didn't mean to do it and he beat me, and he kept saying, "Didn't you mean to do it?" Cursing at me. I said, "No daddy." The licks got harder, so I lied and said yes, I meant to do it. Well, he really got mad he threw me into the dresser. I had a big bruise on my side that was so painful. I was so glad when that episode was finish. I cried myself to sleep. Now my dad always taught me to be afraid of white men. I remember when I was small and Elvis Presley came on the television and me and my stepsisters used to rush to the tv to be the first to kiss him. My dad saw me one day rushing to kiss the tv to give Elvis the big one first. He slapped me so hard I thought my lips had left my face. He cursed me out and told me he better not ever catch me with or dating a white man. He said they were evil and would take me in the woods and kill me. I believed him. He was my dad. I remember sometimes my dad would beat me unmerciful and as soon as he would finish, he would say to me, now you know daddy loves you. That had me confused. I didn't understand why my dad's love was painful, and my aunt's love was hugs and kisses. He would dare me to look at him when he was talking to me. No eye to eye contact. He would say, Don't look at me!!! I should knock your dam eyes out!! He thought I was a lair anyways.

If he asked me if I did anything, I would say no, but he would beat me until I said yes, and then beat me worse. I started thinking about how I could kill him and get away with it. Everything I thought of ended with me going to jail. I thought about stabbing him and put bandages on the stab wounds. I was 12, I didn't know any better. He told me he hated white people and wanted me to do the same. I guess he changed his mind because his next victim was a white woman. I was very puzzled when he introduced her as his lady friend. He tried to explain to me that she had money and that she owned her own business. It was a horse and dog kennel. My brother had returned home to our dad and he really enjoyed riding her horses. I was afraid of them. He had my brother helping her with the cleaning. Of course he didn't like it, but he was tired of being locked in the trunk of the car and the punching. It wasn't long until she started staying every night. She was really nice to us. She had my dad to take us to see my mom. I was sooo excited about that. Looking back now I think my dad wanted my mom to see him with this pretty white lady and we were living good. She would buy me new clothes, I didn't know how to act with something new because it had been so long. Our clothes were from the thrift store. I remember each time we visited my mom, my cousin and my nieces would try to hide me from my dad when it was time for me to leave. I would tell them how my dad was beating on us and they would cry with me. My dad found me hiding and I was crying telling my mom I didn't want to go back and for some reason, she wasn't listening. My dad was so mad with me that he beat the blood out of me for hiding. He threw me into the corner end of the dresser. He told me that I wasn't going back to see her if I tried to hide again. Maybe once or twice he took me on his big motorcycle to see my mom to show off his new bike. I got off that thing walking like a bowlegged cowgirl. Well later in the relationship they started arguing a lot. One day my dad went to work, and this lady told me that she was going to Miami to pick up a friend of hers.

    When she returned home with this lady, she was black. They both went into my dad's bedroom. I was sitting on the couch watching tv and she came out the bedroom with this sheer thin pretty outfit. She went to the kitchen and got something to drink, and went back in the bedroom. Her and the black lady stayed in there until my dad came home. They were in there in the nude lying in each other arms. My dad called me to the door so that I could see them. He told me to go sit in the living room. Next thing I heard was a lot of tumbling and cursing. He beat them both and threw her out. I was so nervous for so long. I developed nail biting then skin biting. He eventually went back to her because she had a son from him later after that happen. Well that left me and my brother, and dad made three. He taught me how to clean the houses, cook his food and have his bath water ready when he got home from work. We continued to work in the fields for him and give him our monies. He bought our clothes from the thrift store once again. When I went to school, I just knew someone recognized their clothes I had on. I hated it and him. The only thing I am grateful of is that he never touched me inappropriately. Never anything sexual with me. My brother built his nerve to run away. He ran to the white lady and she brought him a bus ticket home to my mother. That left me there alone. I was not smart at all in school because I barely went to school. I had so much on my mind that had nothing to do with books. I had a brother that lived with my mom making all A's and in the newspaper every week playing basketball. One day I got detention for chewing gum in class and my dad had just picked up a newspaper reading the article on his son playing that ball. I can remember what he was saying as he was beating me, "Your brother over there making something of his self and you over here bull shitting. You ain't shit and never will be shit, you will never have shit, or a good husband and he will be ugly as hell if you do get one." I think I got a little upset with my brother that day and he had no idea what was happening to me. He threw me in the air and hit me coming down. I don't know how but he mastered that. He threw me onto the furniture. He didn't care where I landed. I had a friend that lived down the street with her mom, dad and brother. She was truly a blessing just to talk to. We were the same age, but I let her know what was happening to me. Her mom was a sweetheart, I remember she used to sew and make my friend a lot of short sets from the material of the flour bag. They were so pretty, I remember her making me a few. I loved her so much. I was like her second daughter. I used to cry to my friend and her mom and at least she would listen. People was afraid to get involved same as today.

Chapter 4

THE FIRST TIME

One day my friend's cousin came over to visit and I was there. Our eyes locked and it was love at first sight for me. What did I know about love. Don't know. I just had this funny feeling running through my body. Only person I knew for sure I loved was my brother and that 1 stepsister I needed to rescue from all that pain she was getting physically and mentally. I was a virgin and he already had a baby at 14.(I didn't know this at the time.) I was so in love with him because he told me how pretty I was and how much he liked me. I had never had a like, like that! It didn't take long for me to give in to having sex with him. The first time was awful. I threw him off me onto the floor. I told him that I was sorry, but I didn't know what to expect. He was very humbled and said, "That's okay, I understand." That was the end for that day. I was so scared to go home I just thought some way my dad would know just by looking at me. I was wrong. He didn't even notice! The next time was the very next day. (All smiles) It was to me the best sex I had ever had. Only it was the only sex I had ever had. (laughing) We were inseparable. I started school and I learned that he was the big man on campus. Great in sports, and great with the girls. He used to walk with me to my classes. He would give me this big kiss before he left for his class. I thought I had died and went to heaven. I started hearing humors about him and another girl seeing each other. I didn't care because he treated me like a princess. And of course I watched my dad cheat on his wife and girlfriends, and only because he was my first, but I wasn't his first, hell I wasn't even his 3rd. We would catch the school bus back to my house some days and to his mother's house some days. I was very sexually active. I didn't know anything about douches or how to clean the inside of me out. I used to stick a wash cloth up me thinking that was how I clean my vagina out. He started out using condoms but that didn't last long. I was only 14. I didn't know, but I knew my dad would kill us both if he knew I was having sex. At school I joined the modern dance group. I loved dancing and was the best at it. I was so good that my instructor made me the girl leader out of 20 something girls. Then you had your guy leader. He and I created our own dances and then we had group dances. My dad was so mad about that. He made me go to work for about 3 weeks straight. The school was wondering why I wasn't in school. He told them I was sick. He told me I wasn't going to live free on him. I was working in his house. After the concern of the school, he sent me back. I was so happy because I loved dancing and I miss going to my boyfriend mom's house from school. One day they invited the news reporters to come out and tape our dances and we could invite our family. I told him about it and he told me I wasn't going to be in it. I snuck out the window and ran to catch the school bus. I did it. When I got home, I got one of the worse beatings I had ever gotten from him. In the mist of all the work and abuse I was still sneaking with my love and working. One day after school we went to this drug house and everyone was smoking marijuana. He asked me to try it and I did. After we left there we went back to my house and had the best sex we had ever had. I was already in so much pain until marijuana made me numb. Well my dad found out about the boyfriend and the taping at the school. So, he decided to enroll me in karate classes. I hated it. I was the only black person there. We had a jamboree at school and I was supposed to be there to perform all the dances with the group and the dances me and the guy leader created together. My dad said I couldn't go. I wanted to kill him or myself. He told my dance instructor I had an appointment somewhere else. The karate instructor told him I didn't have to come on that day I could come the next week. I said, "Daddy, I have the jamboree and they are depending on me to be there." He said, "Shut up and you do what I say." He told the karate instructor I would be to class. I wanted to run away and go to the jamboree, but it was at night and the school was probably 20 miles from my house. I cried a river for a whole week. When they came on television with Fame, I felt as though I should have been Debbie Allen. I had so much good talent in dancing, that was my get away. That Wednesday night he took me to karate class and I didn't do anything they asked me to do. I just wanted to die. My dad didn't care about my feelings. After I got tired of those kids kicking my butt, I decided it was time to learn how to fight back. Then, I thought maybe one day it would come in handy to kick my dad's butt. He had built up so much fear in me until I knew not to try him physically. I moved up fast to black belt because every time I hit or kick something or someone, I thought of him. My boyfriend decided he wanted to talk to my dad about dating me. I begged him not to, but he did it anyway. He never knew about the abuse because my dad dared me to tell anyone. My dad talked to him real nice, but told him no way, no how, he was allowing me to date him or anyone else. He shook his hand and sent him on his way. I was so scared because my dad was too calm with him. After he left, he told me, "I should kick your ass." I backed up in a corner because I know if he said I should, he was. He said you date who and when I say so. He walked up to me and told me to go to bed. As I was walking away, he took my head and slammed my face into the brick wall. I scream and cried all night. I prayed that I would die! I couldn't go to school the next day because when I looked in the mirror, I didn't recognize who I was. My dad left for work and I ran to his ex-wife's house who I still thought of as my mother. She looked at me and she called the school and told them what happened to me. The dean of girls asked her if I could be in her office the next morning, and she said yes. I don't recall how I got there but I was there. When I walked in there all mouths dropped to the floor. They could not believe that my dad did that to me. The dean had called the Child Protected Services and they asked me to remove my clothes. They were shocked to see all the bruises all over my body. I told them that if my dad found out that they knew, he would kill me. I told them everything mostly about how he locked my brother in the trunk of his car. CPS lady told me to go back home and pretend nothing happened with them. She said if he ever threaten you saying, he's going to hit you, I want you to run and call me to let me know where you are. She gave me her phone number. I felt good about that, somebody finally listen. My dad doctored on my face, so I could heal to get back to work. The next week on a school day he looked at me and told me to go to work. I asked him if I could go to school and he said, "No!!!" He looked at me with that look and said, "If you don't go to work, I will tear your ass up when I get home!!" I put on my work clothes and went up front street and all the kids started laughing at me. The work bus and school bus was loading up the same place and around the same time. I started crying and ran home. I was so scared until I was shaking. I started biting my nails and I thought about running away. I remember the lady told me to run and call her. I had told my best friend about seeing this lady and what she said to me.

Somehow, my friend must have been telling her mom everything, because that day everything fell in place. Her mom had already talked to a lady about me running to her house if I had to. I made my break out, scared as ever. My best friend took me by the hand and we ran together crying. She took me to this lady and her husband's house that was not too far from my dad's house, but far enough for him not to know where I was. She let me in with opened arms. I gave her the number that the CPS lady gave me, and she called her to let her know I had run away. The CPS lady asked her if it was ok if I lived there until they figured things out. I was happy for a little while there until I found out they had a different religion than I was used to. I had to study my books all day Friday. Church was on a Saturday, and no meat. When they went to work, I used to sneak my boyfriend in their back door. He was my peace and yet he still didn't know the magnitude of what I was going through. All he cared about was getting me in bed.

Well my dad never knew where I was, that was the best thing out of all while living with them. Christmas was coming up and my mom came looking for me to bring me home with her for the holidays. My brother showed her where my dad lived and that's when she found out that I had run away. The CPS people had already got in touch with my dad and let him know that they knew where I was, and that he was not to come around me, but they never told him where I was.

When my mom came, my dad called CPS and told them that my mom wanted to see me and they got a sheriff to bring her to me. I was so surprised to see her and my brother. When that door open, I jumped into my momma's arms. The sheriff walked in and last but not least, my dad came in. I ran and balled up in a knot in the corner and started screaming NO!!! NO!!!!!!! It was as though I had seen a MONSTER. He said, "There go daddy baby." I was shaking and crying. I looked at my mom and she was crying. The sheriff grabbed me up and said to me. "You don't have to be afraid of him, I'm not going anywhere." He said, "I promise I won't leave you." My dad tried to hug me saying he missed me. All I could see is my momma. She talked to the lady and asked her if she could take me home for the Christmas holiday and the CPS lady said yes. She had to bring me back for court. I left with my mom. When I got back, I had missed my boyfriend so much until I was ready to come back. I continued sneaking him in these people house, having sex, until someone in the neighborhood told her they saw him coming in and out of her house. She came to me fussing about it, so I ran away from her too. I had another friend who lived with her aunt not too far from her house. So, I ask her to please ask her aunt if I could stay there with them. The meanest looking lady in the neighborhood said "Yes." We called the CPS lady and I told her that I had ran away again. She said "Carletha, when are you going to stop running?" I just cried. I was tired of the church thing, the not eating certain foods, couldn't go anywhere, couldn't have any friends over, t v off at dawn and most of all no boyfriend. Oh my God, I had so much freedom and so much fun. She let us go to school dances and hang outside. There was a lady that lived across the street from her aunt house that had a nephew that come home from the Army. It never dawned on me that he was so much older than me. As the courts was trying to decide what to do with me at the age of 15, I was having sex and smoking weed any chance I got. I heard humors that my boyfriend had got another girl pregnant, so I was mad. I started sleeping with the army man across the street, how convenient. He was so sweet and knew how to handle a lady. My boyfriend came to tell me that he loved me, and that he stopped seeing the other girls. I left with him that evening and we smoked weed and had sex. I went to school the next day and my friend showed me the girl that was saying she was pregnant. I was so mad that I said enough is enough. I kept sleeping with the army man. Now when people said she was pregnant from my boyfriend I start saying, "So what, I'm pregnant too!!" But I was just saying it so it could

A Cry for Help

get back to her. I was still very much in love with my boyfriend. Then the time came for me to go to court. They charged my dad with child abuse, but he didn't go to jail or anything. He sat there and told the judge that he never hit me, and that he always brought me nice things. He found jewelry that my aunt sent me from NY for my birthday and presented it to the judge and claimed he brought it. My mother came and my brother, the proud son, the basketball player and one of my other brothers. My dad had told the courts that my mom was nothing but a drunk and slept with men over her kids. So, they did not want me with neither of them. They were discussing putting me in a foster home at 15. The judge asked me about the beatings, and he asked me to explain. I told him that I think maybe you spank your kids but not fight them as if you hate them. Then my brother asked if he could speak, the basketball player. The judge said, "Yes." He said I lived with my mom all my life and I finished school and I have 3 scholarships to go to college. He said I never been in any kind of trouble. He said this because my brother that was being beaten by our dad had been in and out of the boy's home. And they told the judge I had a sister that lived in Bakersfield, California. So, the judge made his decision to let me go with my mom, but I had to go to California to live with my sister for a year to keep my dad from coming to Palm Beach County. They were afraid he may kidnap me or kill me after putting him through all of this. When I got home with my mom, she put me in school until my sister was able to come get me. All I did in school was sleep. I was not trying to go leave my mom to go live with a sister and her family that I barely remembered. All I knew was she is my momma's daughter. My brother heard me telling my mom I did not want to leave and go to California. He said to me that if I didn't go, he would call the judge or my dad and let them know I was still in Florida. My mom called my sister and she caught the bus to Florida and bought me a ticket to go back with her. It took 3 days on that darn bus. I started throwing up the whole trip. When we got to California my sister took me to have a pregnancy test. I was pregnant at 15! I was miserable only because I knew that I was pregnant, and the father was thousands of miles away. And he had no idea that I was pregnant. My sister tried to get assistance for me but when the courts sent my dad a child support letter, he told them that he wasn't my father. He said my father's name was Calvin

Brown only because I was in my mother maiden name. See he never signed my birth certificate. My mom told me that he told her if she had any more children that he would leave her, and she was already pregnant with me. She said when he found out, HE LEFT HER! I cried at least 300 nights. I was a cry baby. My daughter was born two months after my 16th birthday. My sister was at school, so her husband took me to the hospital because I was having pain and pushing. When I got to the hospital, they checked me, and I was dilating. I told the nurse I had to go to the bathroom. It felt as if I had to poop. I was sitting on the toilet pushing and something told me to feel down between my legs. When I touched it, it felt like a big round ball was hanging out of me. I ran and told the nurse something big was hanging out of me. She rushed me to the table and looked and scream for assistant. She said my baby was coming out in the water bag. They said my baby was born with a veil on her face. A very gifted and smart child. They put me to sleep and I didn't feel a thing. I had a baby girl in 1971. I was so happy because I had someone to love and love me back. She was all mine and the only way I could lose her was if I didn't treat her right. There was no way that was going to happen. All I could think about was the day I get back to my man and let him know that I had a daughter from him. The day came sooner than I thought. My baby was no more than 2 months old when we left California. We were Florida bound. My dreams I was having was finally coming into reality.

    The whole family moved back home to Florida. I moved in with my mom who only had two rooms. Not a two bedroom, (two rooms). The first room had a bedroom/living room. The back room had a smaller bed in it where the clothes hung over your head on clothes hanger wires twisted together. She had a hot plate that she cooked on. My mom cooked on it and the food was delicious. She had a small cooler for a refrigerator. No inside bathroom. The bathroom was down the walk way. It was for that whole floor of people. It was scary. It had 3 toilets in it and the big giant shower made of brick. It was full of cock roaches and big spiders. My mom used to use a foot tub, (small bucket to urinate in at night.) Sometimes she used it to bath in too. I didn't care.

    I was just happy to be home. I kept my promise to my sister that I would come back for her. I went to get her and brought her back with me to Belle Glade, Florida for a visit. She said I came to get her just in time because she was thinking about killing herself. Thank you God, for saving her. I never really thought about my mom being a stranger to me too. I just knew I was with the mom I've always cried for. My grandmother who was her mother lived next door to her and my Aunt. Her sister lived down stairs around the corner in the next building. My mother's cousin lived up on the third floor and she had one of my nieces living with her. My oldest brother lived across the street and so did the next oldest brother with his wife and son. My oldest brother had another daughter who was living on the other side across the street with her boyfriend. I was in a new world. If only I knew that all hell was about to break through and my life would never be the same. I knew my grandmother didn't like me, but she loved my daughter. My mother didn't like me because she didn't know me. I was a stranger to them also. One thing that was true was they loved to drink. My grandmother and my aunt drank gin and my mom loved her beer. My grandmother was a drunk. She stayed drunk. At that time Belle Glade was like a big work camp, but a very small town. People came there to work in the fields. All you had there was field work; celery, corn, and sugar cane, drugs, gambling and a night club on every corner. There was no Macdonald's or Burger King or anywhere to shop. You had to ride to West Palm Beach, FL to really shop. I had a big gap in the front of my teeth. I hated it. I asked my mom if I could go to work with her to make money for me and my baby. I started working in the celery field packing celery along with my mom. I didn't mind working because I was used to it, only this time the money was mine. Some days I would leave the fields early because of cold weather.

    My mom used to fuss at me, but I didn't care. I hate cold weather. I told her I needed to go to the bathroom which was an outhouse in the field. When she saw me again, I was waving bye to her in one of the trucks going to town. She would curse me out when she got home, but at least she wasn't hitting me. I promised myself that I would never work in another field as long as I can help it, no matter what I had do to survive for myself and my children, that little money! My mom only had one brother and she hadn't seen him in years since they were young. He came from NY living with their first cousin. He was a drunk also. One day my mom was at work and he came next door where I was and ask me to give him a hug. I went to hug him, and he tried to kiss me in my mouth. I pushed him, and he grabbed me trying to hold my face to his. He was trying to put his tongue in my mouth. We fell on the bed and I was kicking and screaming. He was asking me to stop screaming and just give him a kiss. We both fell on the floor. When he heard my grandma asking what was going on as she was coming next door to my mom's house, he told me that I better not say nothing!! As soon as my mom got home from work, I told her what happened. He told her that I was lying and that was the end of that. After that I just always tried not to be around him if I was alone.

Chapter 5
ANOTHER GIFT FROM GOD

My brother's wife had a handsome brother that used to come visit them. I started visiting them a little more often, and so did he. We started talking and one thing lead to another. I was crazy about him, but I was still in love with my other baby's father in Ft Pierce. I heard rumors that a niece of mine was liking my new boy friend. She was already living with her boyfriend, but it was convenient for her too. She was my brother's niece. Her boyfriend would never know. She used to hang with her boyfriend's sister all the time, so I didn't think she was after my boyfriend! I asked him to tell me what was going on and he said to me "nothing." He told me that when she came over that she flirts with him, but he wasn't returning the favor. After I kept hearing the rumors about them, I cheated on him with a friend of my brother's, the basketball player. His friend was a basketball star also. I only slept with him twice. I ended it because I was falling in love with my boyfriend. I was young, and I wanted to believe him. I was in so much pain, mentally. I was crazy about him, but was skeptical about the rumors. She was my niece, for God's sake!! My grandmother was more upset with me about the situation. She was screaming at me saying I was nothing but a whore and a liar!!! Oh, and a Red Bitch. She was saying this while my mom was talking to me about my niece and me. She said that he was lying to me and my mom told me that they didn't sleep with each other. He kept saying it was not true. I guess my grandma was still upset that I told the truth on her son. I don't know why because nothing was done about it!! I continued to have sex with him until I needed to get away. I left town and finally went back to Ft Pierce to see my ex-stepmother, my stepsisters, and two brothers that was my father's sons. I took my daughter to my ex-boyfriend mother's house, and it was just like I had dreamed it. He answered the door and by his surprise there stood me and his daughter. He was shocked. His mother came to the door and welcomed us in with open arms. I thought I was dreaming. He asked so many questions like, where have you been, all this time? And what happen to make me leave town. All I wanted to do was throw him down and screw him to death. But his mom was there and his sister. They played with my daughter while he and I went on their front porch to talk. I left there, and I went back to my stepmother's house and was feeling sick I was throwing up once again, but was still having my period. I just couldn't be pregnant. I wanted my ex in Ft Pierce back. Yes, I was pregnant. When I found out I was already 6 ½ months into the pregnancy. I went back home to my mother's house and I had to break the news to everyone. All hell broke loose. My mom was mad that I was on my second child and could hardly take care of the first one. I didn't know what to do, so my baby's father asked his mom if it would be okay if I moved in with them. We were hanging out in this place one night. Just my niece and some friends, and that's when she said out loud, "My man's name is… ..,but my boyfriend name is……." So, I looked at her. She was talking about my baby daddy. She said when I left, they really became close. That's when I broke the news that I was pregnant from him. She tried everything to stop this move-in from happening. But, I was pregnant, and my mom was pissed at me, cursing me out and telling me I was not bringing two babies in her house/ rooms. I left. His mom had a beautiful home with a bathroom inside the house and it was big. They lived in a town about twelve miles from where my mom was. His mom had her family there. She had a big beautiful home and her own kids. Next door it was a family there that she had a lot of kids too. I used to come and go a lot and it was this little boy around 12 or 13 that used to just stare at me. One day he wanted to give me a hug because I was leaving. He said to me, "I may not see you again." My niece started a rumor saying that my second child's daddy was not the father of my baby that the guy I cheated with was her father. But he didn't want to hear that. We knew she was jealous. She used to throw rocks at me. I would always say, "Just wait." I caught them together a lot. She hung with some of his family that didn't like me, and it was some that loved me. Of course, I was having his first child. I told her to wait until I have my baby. I would give her a good fight. She just always talked trash about that's not his baby and they were still seeing each other. Finally, on April 1st my water broke that night in bed. I thought I had peed in the bed because my water never broke with my first baby. I stayed at my mom's house to be with my other daughter. I was back and forth because I never wanted her to miss me like I missed my mom. I had to walk about 3 miles the next morning to the clinic to get checked. They checked me, and my water had broken the night before. They told me I needed to get to the hospital. The hospital was 12 miles from where I was. I had to walk back 3 miles to my mom's house and get a ride to the hospital. I was in pain but not a lot of pain. When I got to the hospital, they rushed me back. The doctor told me that my baby was early, and it was small. He told me that I would have to bare the pain because, there wasn't nothing they could give me. He said it was a 50/ 50 chance of losing me or her or both of us. He said I had to stay awake and just follow instructions. He said, "You don't mind having pain for your baby, do you?" I said, "No, I don't mind." I was so scared. I never had my mom there beside me when having my babies. It didn't take long for little momma to come into this world. She was small and beautiful. She had to remain in the hospital for a few weeks to gain more weight. I went back to my mom's house to recover. I was back and forth to the hospital to see my daughter. While at home with my mom she kept telling me that I was not bringing two babies in her house. She was doing some cursing and fussing. I cried because I wanted my baby with me. I went back to my boyfriend's mother house with my baby while my mom had my first daughter. One of my boyfriend relatives came and told me that my baby father was with my niece. They took me where they were laughing and talking. I cursed him out and told him that me and my baby would be gone when he got home. I never left, so when he came home, he had her in the car with him. I went out to the car and told him I was tired of his shit, all the lying sleeping with the aunt and the niece. And she was still living with her boy friend. When I said I was tired of this shit to him, she said she was tired of this shit too. I said to her "I was not talking to you!" It was time for the fight she always wanted with me. I was more than happy to fight her. I wanted to show her who the aunt was. After they broke us up, I went upstairs and packed my things and my baby. My momma was giving me hell. She was yelling, "How you gonna take care of two damn children." She stressed that I better do something because she didn't have enough room for us. My baby father's mother came to talk to me about her keeping my baby and she said her son didn't have anything to do with the conversation we were having. She promised me that whenever I got ready to get my baby it would not be a problem. She said, "You are young, and I know one day you may settle down and get married or just want your baby, you can get her." She said her son would not have a say in the matter. So, I let my baby go to give her a better life. Every time I saw my daughter, his mom had her beautiful. She was living like a little queen.

I started hanging out with friends smoking weed, just having random sex. A few years later the town was like a baby Vegas. You had nothing but high rolling gamblers, drug dealers and dealings, pimps and want to be pimps. Even I wanted to be a pimp. I wanted to pimp men and if they didn't obey me, I would be allowed to beat them physically. There was a club or hole in the wall on every corner. Where we lived, you would walk downstairs, and everything was available to you. All the young men were running after older women and all the older men were chasing young girls. They didn't care about their family at home and didn't care about how much money they had to pay to sleep with a young girl. There was also a lot of raping happening too. I heard that my niece left her boyfriend and moved in with my baby's father in his mom house. The last thing I wanted is for her to be around my baby. I got so depressed that I started snorting cocaine and smoking marijuana almost every day. I was convinced that my mom hated me too. I didn't have to worry about either one of my daughters because one was home with me and my mom and the other one was with her grandmother. I was eighteen with two children, living on welfare and no role models to follow. I started dating women's husbands, for money of course. I only slept with the biggest pockets, the drug kings.

Big money men, men that I knew were clean and had a lot of class. My mom always reminded me that my p...y was made for money and not to give it away free like I was doing. I learned quick how to ask for money, so I would not hear her saying, "All you do is go out and F these men and bring home nothing but a wet ass. You can't even buy a bar of soap to wash your stinking ass, and you got a baby to take care of." I moved up fast because I was bow legged and a small waist with nice size hips, and I was cute. My hair was so long I had a big afro. I dyed my hair gold. I worked in the celery field and got my mouth fixed. Put a gold tooth to close my gap between my teeth and wore a neck and arm full of gold jewelry. Every day I wore 6inch high heels. My new name was Goldie. I was very sexy, and I meant to be. That was my way to come up. I thought somehow, I could master how to make my vagina feel so good, and it would be a plus that I always knew how to wind my body. I learned how to work the muscles everywhere. I knew it was good because everybody told me so, and I always left them, they never left me. And when I stopped seeing them, they either cried and begged me not to leave them or wanted to hurt me physically or tried to pay me to stay. One thing everyone knew was that when I was finished with you, I was finished. I was a spoiled hot mess, by men. Some of the men I was dealing with had a wife or girlfriends living with them and they wanted to leave them for me. I was not having that, I didn't want them!! That was not the love I was looking for, but it was the only love I thought I had. I forgot all about prayer and GOD. I HATED MYSELF AND EVERYONE EXCEPT MY GIRLS. Soon some of my friends started looking strange. Their bodies were drying up and no one knew why. Soon they were dying. Soon as they showed Rock Hudson on the news with HIV, that's when we knew that's what our friends were dying with. No one knew how it was being spread at that time. We all thought it was from homosexual men only. Because that's what the news was saying. But I had girlfriends dying and I knew they were straight. It was very, very scary and hurtful. I know that I had to change from seeing men for what they had to dating drug dealers. Selling drugs was just as worst but that was a step up for me. I tried to go see my daughter every weekend. I would catch rides there. One night my mom was fussing at me telling me what somebody said about me using drugs etc… she said I wasn't shit. I told the niece I was closed to that I was tired of living and I was going take a bottle of pills. She thought I was joking. My mom was in the other room I took one pill after another one. I took about 15 pills. Don't know what kind they were but the whole room turned red. I felt as if I was walking on clouds. My mom called the police and from there I was taken to the hospital. They pumped my stomach and put IV fluids in my body. I stayed overnight and was sent home. Nothing changed it was just like it never happen. My quest continued. I remember my friends and I used to sneak in the clubs because we weren't of age yet. I admired the women who were well dressed and had their drink in front of them and a cigarette in their hand. I thought that was amazing. I couldn't wait until it was my turn, so that I could look like that. I myself, I loved to dance, and I could dance!!! I knew all the men were watching this star!! The men loved me, and most of the women that didn't know me hated me. I could care less. I dared any of them to say anything to me, with just the look on my face. I had a few fights here and there and I had a reputation of being crazy and didn't mind giving you a good fight. I inherited the look my dad use to give us. And learned a new language called cursing. One of my friends told me she heard someone saying Carletha don't play about her kids, her money and her men. I laughed and said, "Damn right!!"

Chapter 6

TORTURED

I was raped by two different men. The first time was a friend of my boyfriend at the time. He was a big man. I was eighteen years old. My boyfriend and I used to use his room to meet and have sex. His room was in an alley inside of a building. This night he told me that my boyfriend was there waiting on me and that he would walk me there, so I would be safe. Once we entered the room it was no one there. He pushed me on the bed and tore my clothes off me. I was screaming but no one could hear me. He pulled out this weapon he made of clothes hangers and hit me with it and told me to shut the hell up. He raped me and all I could do was cry. When he finished, I told him I needed to go to the bathroom which was outside his room down the hall.

He went with me there will the hangers in his hand and dared me to scream. I thought I could make a run for it, but I couldn't. He stood right there as I peed. He grabbed me by the arm and took me back to the room where he raped me again and beat me. He got a pleasure out of hitting me and raping me at the same time. When he finished, he told me if I told anyone that he would kill me. I told him to please kill me physically because I was already dead mentally. He started telling me how sorry he was and begging me not to say anything, after I asked him to kill me. I promised that I would keep quiet because all I wanted to do was leave. He had the nerve to walk me home still saying how sorry he was. On the way, I ran into my uncle and I told him what had just happen and at the same time this cop I was sleeping with came up in his patrol car. I screamed for him to stop. The man who raped me ran. They tried to find him but from what I heard he ran all the way to NY. They say they had been trying to catch him for a long time.

They heard he was raping young girls but could never prove it. When I got to the hospital, they check me and saw that I had been sexually active but couldn't prove that I had been raped until they saw the bruises where he had hit me. But he was gone. The second rape was by a best friend that hung out in our circle of friends. He was a big fat guy, but nice, I thought. I needed to go see my daughter and he volunteered to take me. It was twelve miles and in between that ride, was nothing but cane fields, which they used to call the green top motel and it was free. He took me to see my baby, and on the way back he turned into the cane field and said to me, " Fuck or walk." I was so hurt because he was our friend and I had to look at him every day. Most of all, my period was on and he didn't even care. He tore my panties off and he raped me. I was afraid to fight because the last time I had gotten beaten so bad. So, I gave in and let him have his way. How do you get raped and you enjoy it? I think because the first time I was beaten and raped, so I focused more on giving in than fighting. I only told my niece that lived with my mom's cousin because her boyfriend and he were best friends for years. I knew he liked me, but he also knew, that would be the only way that he could have me. I was thinking what more could happen. I was numb just living day by day. The next guy I met put a gun to my head with one bullet in the chamber because I found out he was cheating on me and shooting drugs in his arm and we were living together. He had been in prison and to him it was love at first sight, so I tried to have a real relationship with him. He was very handsome and built well from head to toe. To me and every other woman he was new meat in town, even though he was from there. He had been in prison from a young man. We got an apartment together. That lasted about 5 months. I had no problem with you selling drugs, you just couldn't use them, not at that magnitude. I left him and moved in with my mom and my daughter. After he put the gun to my head and pulled the trigger twice, he heard my mom's voice, and he dared me to move so I just sat there, I had no fear in me. My heart was like a brick. He ran away from the house. I went and brought me a gun and

I told my mom whenever I see him, I was going to kill him. She called my dad and asked him if I could live with him until I calm down. I can't even tell you how miserable I was there. He used to always take me around to these old men and talk like he wanted me to date them. I guess he wanted to pimp me too. I would just say nice to meet you. He would always say they own this, and they own that. I could care less. At that time, I went by my first daughter father's house and his mom told me that he had joined the Air Force. I was shocked because the last thing I had heard was that he was hanging out pimping and using hard drugs. But he had made it out of the streets. I was so happy to hear that. Then his mom said he had to deny a lot of children and your daughter was one of them. I said, "What!!" She said when he joined every woman that thought she had his baby went to child support. I was hurt, but then I thought, she might not be his anyway. I was seeing the Army man at the same time, even more. I was free to come home after the news was all over town that the boyfriend who put the gun to my head tried to rob a bread truck and got shot in the head. He didn't die but we knew he would be in prison for a long time. He was the reason I got hit in the head in a night club by one of his ex girlfriends. I gave her a beat down in the movie theater prior to her sneaking up behind me and busting my head open in the club. I had my gun in my purse but left it with a friend, so I could dance. I was running and bleeding like a hog. She stayed hidden for a long time. I was always carrying a gun and people knew that I would use it. If they didn't know, I knew. I would have shot her. During all this pain and aggravation, my baby brother was spending his life in and out of jail. So in between me taking care of myself I was taking care of him also. I made sure he didn't need or want for anything, in or out of jail. Only thing, he was in more than he was out.

I cried so much for my daughter to be home with me, but my mom kept reminding me that she was in a better place. She kept saying if I took her that her family was going to double team me and beat me so bad that they may kill me, because we heard that they had beat a cousin of mine and knocked his teeth out with a board. He was also married to one of their family members. So, I continued to visit her and sometimes my niece would bring her to town with her. One day

I heard my daughter called her ma. I was so mad. I took my daughter from her and told her you are not her mom and she won't be calling you ma. I cursed her father out when I saw him. Remember my brother was married to his sister. Two or three years later she had a son which she named him after my daughter's father. Only he looked just like her ex boyfriend. My daughter's father signed his birth certificate as his father, so I guess legally he was his son. I had to swallow that because you know she was happy to let me know that. Anyways, life goes on. Only now for the rest of my life, I had to live with people asking how's that his sister if you are her momma and his auntie. Her father begged me every time he saw me, and I used to sleep with him behind her back but that got old with me and I was no longer wanting to be in that circle. I wanted that chapter of my life to be over because now there were children involved. That was the best decision I had ever made.

I met this tall handsome fine man. He was much older than me. He sold drugs big time. He used to have me holding his money as he made it. I thought I was rich. I had never seen that much money in my life. I knew I had to tie him down with this good stuff. The first time we made love, yes made love, (I had never made love before), he told me that he was a freak. My understanding of a freak was someone who shot drugs in their system. That's what they taught me in school that a freak was. He whispered that in my ear as he was on top of me. I was so into him. I said I don't care. He gently kissed me from head to toe then came back up and stopped in the middle. I had never felt anything in the world that felt that good. When that feeling came over me, I blanked out and saw nothing but stars. (seriously). I was head over heels in love with him and he knew it. We would follow each other like bee after honey. We were crazy in love.

He thought I was cheating, and I thought he was cheating. He was so jealous because now I'm like a superstar. I stayed dressed up, hair always beautiful. He had created a monster. I entered a lot of best dressed contest and won a lot of them. If I didn't win, my favorite niece won. We also entered a lot of best dance contest, all in the clubs. My daughters were living good and I was finally happy. But I couldn't let go of my past. One night I was out and the owner of a night club liked me and he knew it. He walked in and saw us talking and assumed we were making plans to be with each other. He took me home and tied my hands behind my back with wire clothes hangers. And sodomized me. That was torture!!!!!! I hated him, for a little while. My trust was leaving because my dad had cheated on all his women even if they were good women. My man had 2 children from someone else and their mother was still crazy about him, so she never wanted me to come with him to see them but didn't mind me babysitting. I found out a couple of times I kept their children that they were at a hotel together. Once I heard that, and as soon as he stepped in the door, I cursed him out and he said he was sorry. That let me know that it was true. He told me that she was using the kids to be with him. I picked up a butcher knife and I threw it as he ran from me. The wooded part of the knife hit him in the back. I wanted the actual sharp end to stick him. When I tell you, this man was a freak, he was a freak!! I used to be asleep and he would wake me up with toothpaste burning me between my legs or ice or fruits. If I didn't have sex with him, he would cry and beg me all night until I gave in. One night he saw me coming out of an alley and he just knew I had cheated on him with someone, "I did" He wanted to make love to me and I refused. I had been with someone who knew oral sex just as good as him. And I taught him everything he knew. "I loved oral sex." My man hit me so hard in my nose that the bone was knocked over to the other side. I looked in the mirror. It was broken. He start crying saying he was sorry. All I wanted to do was leave and go to the hospital. My nose was broken and he was crying harder than me. He went into the kitchen and got a knife and repeated over and over, I'm sorry. Then he started stabbing himself in the wrist. I forgot about my nose and was trying to stop him. A large amount of blood shot out of his wrist like a faucet. I got really scared for him. All he kept saying was, I'm sorry, I'm sorry! We both had to go to the hospital. The doctor said he just did miss that main vein in his wrist. I had to go to a specialist for my nose. The specialist told me that he could just push the bone back over as much as possible or he would have to shoot me in the face with a needle to numb my face, but it was going to hurt worst. "I hate needles." I told him to push. I screamed and cried. But my man was there to hold my hand. Time went on and we forgave each other and back in love again. We were the talk of the town, good and bad. I wanted to know about the drug game, (how to get it and how to sell it).

I even set in the room when he had drug addicts testing the dope for him. I watched them shoot that poison in their arms and dose off and scratch at the same time. I had no heart. All I saw was money. I knew I would never do that. One reason, I was too cute and had a reputation to withhold. And I hated needles. And I would never let my daughters see me looking like that. He didn't want me selling drugs, he just wanted me to stay pretty while he made the money, so I start hanging in the club having fun dancing, I always loved to dance. My niece that was living with my baby's father left him and started hanging out with her sister and I clubbing. I did, because she was my brother's daughter. I always tried to be the bigger person because I was her aunt. We had our own little circle of friends. There was another circle of friends that all of us used to be friends, but it's like we split up right down the middle. Her sister told her about a problem she was having with a girl on the other team and it started a big feud between us and them. We met up one night and it was an argument going on with my niece that hung with me, and the sister jumped in the middle and pulled a knife out of her bra. The other girl pulled out a small gun and shot my niece in the neck. (the niece that had my baby's father). I grabbed my niece, and her sister ran screaming calling my mother. I took my niece through an alley where my man saw me and thought I was shot because my clothes was covered in blood. I said help me carry her. She was getting weak and started falling. He grabbed the other side of her and we ran and threw her into a cab and took her to the hospital. While in the cab she scream so loud, and the blood shot up out of her neck like a faucet. I screamed and told her please don't do that again!!! She said, "Ok, ok." She kept saying it was hot and burning. She survived, but the doctor had to leave the bullet in her. Soon she went back to live with my baby's father. My brother, the basketball player, was in NY going to college and playing ball. He didn't know my life. Soon my man and I and his friend got so hot with the police watching us and we thought it was time to leave town. Yes, I had slept with his friend prior to meeting my man. And he was still in love with me. I told them about my aunt and brother in NY. So, we decided we would go there. His friend took his girlfriend with us. We drove to Allentown, PA where a friend of them was living from our home town. It was so cold. I had never experience cold weather like that since I was young living with my aunt. My man had got real comfortable living there. I started complaining because I wanted to go to NY where my family was living. He slapped me and told me to shut up. I slapped him back. I promised after my daddy's abuse, I wasn't going to let another boy or man hit on me and I don't hit them back or try to kill their a.... I told his friend's girlfriend that I was going to call my aunt and ask her to send me a bus ticket. She went back and told him I was trying to sneak away. Our money was running low, and then we found out that their friend was living in an abandon building, and so were we. I was sitting in a chair and I had it leaning back on two legs. I didn't even see it coming. My man hit me from behind with his fist in my face. I hit the floor and he started kicking me. His friend, my ex lover, grabbed him and said, "Man if you kick her again, I will have to kill you." He stopped. He then looked at me and said, "You ain't going no damn where until I'm ready to go." Well the next day the inspectors came by and said we had to leave before they call the police. (Look at GOD) So, we decided to go to NY. I had a black eye and bruised ribs, but I was glad to see my brother and my aunt. Our friend wanted us to go to California, but I was not budging. I got real sassy and told my man to please leave me and go with them because I did not want him anymore. You put your feet on me. That had never happen to me and never will again, not by him anyhow. He started crying saying he didn't want to leave me, and he loved me too much. I told him I hated him and would never love him again. He would not leave. My aunt asked me about my eye and I lied, but she knew he had hit me. She told me since you all are not married you can't live with me. She helped us rent a small apartment closed to where she lived. I was very angry with him. I despised him. To me it was a new town, new meat. Yes, I started sleeping with one of my brother's friends. I didn't care if he saw me or not. I can say I treated him like a dog. My brother got a phone call that my grandmother had died. I thought once we returned home to Florida that he would stay. My aunt's husband drove us down for the funeral and I brought my oldest daughter back with me, and my man refuse to live without me. When I got back to NY, I got a house on housing and food stamps. I moved into a nice apartment, two bedrooms. My aunt helped me furnish it off. Yes, my man was still in NY, but I would not let him move in with me. I told him to keep the previous place we had together. He would come to my place standing outside the door crying and begging me to let him in. I was still angry with him, so I would never let him in. One day he came over and he told me he had some mail for me, so I let him in, he fell on his knees and begged me to take him back. I said no. He went to the kitchen and got a steak knife and just stood there crying. I ran downstairs with my daughter to my brother son's mother and ask her to let her stay there until I call the police for that fool. I explained quickly what was going on and she said, "Ok, go!!!" I ran across the street to my aunt's house and I called the police and explain that he was suicidal and could hurt me and my baby and I was afraid that he may try to kill himself. They said to me, "Miss, if he wants to kill himself, there is nothing we can do." I was shocked!! As I was heading out of the door my brother was running across the street screaming, "Call the ambulance!!!!!!!" He just stabbed himself over and over. I called the police and told them now you can send an ambulance too. When the ambulance brought him down stairs on a stretcher, the steak knife was sticking out of his stomach and he was crying saying, "I want my baby, Carletha!!!" All I could do was cry, because I never wanted this to happen. I just wanted him out of my life. My brother told me when he went up there looking for me, he heard him in my bedroom crying and he said he went in the bedroom and tried to talk to him, but he would not listen. So he tried to take the knife from him. He said he tried so hard until it felt like a bone broke in my ex's hand, so he turned it loose and he stood up and just start stabbing himself. We found out later that my daughter was sent upstairs to see what he was doing by his son's mother. All I could do was hold my daughter and squeeze her and thank God for not allowing that fool to kill my child. I was so mad with him, and I was upset with her for sending a child alone. She was only five years old! My ex told me later that he had slept with my brother son's mother. When I confronted her, she said it was true, but only once. My brother was so hurt, and so was I. I would have never left my daughter with her. I didn't go to the hospital to see him. My brother and my aunt stayed in touch with the hospital. He was in ICU. The doctor said the knife punch a hole in his lung. They had to do an emergency surgery and asked to call his family because they didn't think he would make it through the operation. I called his mom who lived in Florida and I told her what happened and what the doctors said, and she told me that she couldn't leave her job. I could not believe what my ears were hearing. She asked me to please keep her informed. He made it through the surgery but was in ICU for about a week. I still did not want to see him. I figured if he tried to kill himself, the next time it may be him, me and my daughter. I wasn't going to take that chance. My aunt sent for me to come to her house saying she needed to talk to me. When I got there, she asked me to pray for him and to please go see him and stop treating him so bad. She said, "You are the only family he has here, and God was not going to bless you for that." I went to the hospital and I said to him, "The only thing you did was hurt yourself. I still don't want to have anything else in life to do with you." Then I looked at him and said, "Goodbye." He couldn't talk back for the first time, because he was hooked up to so many machines. Around 2am the hospital called my aunt and said he had pulled the tubes out of his mouth and nose and they didn't know if he would live throughout the night. He did. Here comes this Godly woman again wanting to know what I said to him. I told her exactly what I told him. Then she said to me, "You're not going to determine this man death. Whatever he needs to hear from you to live, you will say just that." She said, "He really loves you because he has dying love for you. He would rather die than to live without you. All these beautiful women in his eyesight and he only see's you." I told her, "What he did to himself scared me to death. I have two children." I said, "What if he killed me and my children?" She said, "No, I don't mean for you to stay with him. That's your choice, but get him well so that he can go home to his family." I said, "Yes ma'am". So, I went to the hospital more often and I was friendly, telling him what he needed to hear. I helped him eat and I told him that I loved him. He soon got better and got out of ICU. He was happy, and I was miserable lying to him. He got stronger and stronger, and it was getting closer to him getting out of the hospital, so I called his mom and asked her to send him a plane ticket, so he could come home because he needed her. She asked if she should send 3 tickets, and I said, "No ma'am, just one." When he got out of the hospital we talked, and he begged me to let him perform oral sex on me. As tempting as it was, I couldn't get over the stitches he had from his chest down pass his naval. And I didn't want to confuse him any more than I had already done in the hospital.

I explained to him that his mom had sent him a ticket and he was to leave the next day and I was staying in NY. We cried together and held each other for a long time. I felt so bad for him, but I had to let go for our sake. The next day he left, I cried all that day. It was over after 5yrs of crazy love. My brother left not long after he left NY. He moved back to Florida with my mom. I remained in NY for another year. I moved back to Florida and the first thing I had on my list was seeing my daughter who was with her father's mother. I was tired of all the craziness in the streets, so I decided to get a real job. I was drug free at the time because I never did drugs in NY around my daughter because I wanted to be a real mother. All I did was club here and there and danced all night. It wasn't long before I start hanging out, and I return to smoking marijuana and clubbing when I got home.

Chapter 7

FIRST HUSBAND

I was walking one day, and this man rode up beside me and asked if he could have a word with me. I found out that he was a college graduate and use to play football. He was fine. 250 lbs all muscles, 6'2' dark and handsome. All I saw was hope. This way I can get out of the streets and get my children together in a nice living environment. This man had a great job working with the school board and was drug free. He didn't hang out at all. I started dating him. He had his own apartment and I had my own place. He got so into me that he wanted me to move in with him. That's what I was working on happening, eventually. I needed stability and a change of environment for my girls. I moved in and about 6 months later, we were married. A month after our wedding I was slapped in the face by him and we fought like cats and dogs, because I promised myself after my abuse with my dad, that no man would beat on me again without a fight; no matter what the outcome would be. I was shocked, because I thought he was different. He wasn't a street guy. He was a professional guy. "Just another nightmare." He was very insecure of himself when it came time for us to go to different events. I knew plenty of men, from both worlds, streets and professional. Only this man, I didn't know. I was working at this truck stop restaurant and a man walked in, sat down, and ordered a coke. I was his waitress. He gave me a tip and he left. He called back to the restaurant and asked to speak to me. I got on the phone and he asked me did I see my tip. I told him no. He asked me to look at it. I just put it in my pocket when he gave it to me. It was $50.00. I said, "No!!! I can't take this. You only ordered a drink." He said, "I am long gone, and it is Mother's Day, and you were really nice to me, and I see you work hard." I said, "Thank you and we hung up." I was so excited about it I couldn't wait to tell my husband how nice this man was to me. Oh my God!!! My husband swore I went out and got in this man truck and had sex with him for $50. That is the reason he slapped me. I never told him another nice story like that ever again. He didn't like me hanging with my family. He was tired of my family telling me things about him talking to other women. There were times I caught him with some woman posted up on his car laughing and grinning from ear to ear. There also were rumors about him and his secretary having a fling. I stopped all my cheating while I was married to him. I wanted to be a good wife and really love him and have a family. He decided he wanted a better life for us, so he joined the United States Marine Corp. While the cat's away the mouse will play. We were having problems and physically fighting before he left. I didn't feel bad about cheating. I had to take care of me and I knew how. My special friend was glad he left because that gave him a chance to be with me again and help take good care of me and my daughter while he was gone. One day I couldn't sleep, so I decided to take 2 sleeping pills. I was frying pork chops. I laid on the couch and dosed off to sleep. I jumped up and the whole apartment was full of smoke. I ran to the stove, got a fork, and tried to turn the meat on the other side instead of taking it off. When I stuck the fork in the meat the whole frying pan fell on my left foot. Hot! Hot grease was cooking my foot! The doctor thought he was going to have to cut half or my whole foot off just by looking at it. But, Thank God he didn't. After I got well, I was laughed at for the different colors of my foot. I didn't care. I was just thankful that I had my foot. Well the Marines found out that my husband was behind in child support. Yes, while he was in college, he fathered 3 children and had been married before. That's when I found out too. They gave him an honorable discharge after basic training. He decided he wanted to move to Ft. Lauderdale to get away from my family and his. So, we left and found an apartment in Ft. Lauderdale, FL. One day while visiting my family in Belle Glade, my niece had my daughter with her. My oldest daughter and I cried for my child. I heard my baby call my niece, Ma, and that was the final straw. My daughter said she wanted to go with me. My husband told me to get her and we would take her with what she had on. He said that's your baby and if you want her nobody is going to fuck with you. This was the happiest day of my life. I feared nobody, and I took my baby back with me. We were so happy, "I thought." We even got a dog for the girls. My husband's father was in prison at the time for murder. We would come back home on weekends and visit our family. He would go to the prison to visit his father on Saturday morning then leave there and go visit his girlfriend twelve miles away from the prison. He thought I didn't know about his little affair. And to my surprise, one Saturday he left and told me he was going to see his dad and his stepmother came from visiting him also. I asked her was my husband at the prison with her? She said "No, he never came." I went to my mom's house and got the biggest knife I could find. I jumped in my car to find them. I didn't see them anywhere. When I got back to town, he was standing on the porch of my mother's building. He looked so fresh and clean. I knew he had just taken a shower. I cursed him out and I slapped him. I told him I better not find out he was lying to me, and I told him that I thought that I might be pregnant. We went back home to Ft. Lauderdale. I was so angry because I knew he was lying. When we got home, I continued talking about it and he walked up to me and said, "Shut the hell up!" I told him F you. He then pushed me. I grabbed the iron and hit him across his nose with it. He went in the bathroom, I guess to look at the cut on his nose. As he was coming towards me, and turned around cursing at me, I met him with a gun to his head. My girls was standing there looking, begging me not to kill daddy. They said, "Momma please don't shoot daddy, you will go to jail. Please momma don't kill daddy." I put the gun up and he left the house. I felt so bad that my daughters had to see that. He came home later to talk to me about him having an affair and he kept saying he wanted us to be together. I told him time will tell. "What goes on in the dark will come to the light." He had a good job working with UPS and I was a cashier at a large grocery store. Things were going good for about two weeks and I checked the mailbox and there was a letter in there from his girlfriend. Yes, I opened it. She was telling him about the good love he made to her that day. "Yes, that day I was looking for him." She also said she couldn't wait until he divorced me and marry her, and she would have his baby. She was in college and all this was to happen when she finished. That was the first time I felt I wasn't good enough for him, that he wanted someone on his level. I had cooked dinner and I fixed his food and sat him down to the table to eat. I was smiling, and then I gave him a kiss. He began to eat his food. I walked in the bedroom and got the letter. I then walked into the kitchen and slapped him in the face with the letter. He jumped up and hit me, and we started fighting. My children were in the bedroom. I went towards the kitchen and grabbed a knife, and I told him if he hit me because of his wrong doing, that I would cut him to short to shit!! He threw his hand up at me and I thought he was going to hit me. The knife went straight through his fingers and blood poured out on the floor.

He ran in the bedroom. I knew he had a shot gun in there, so I grabbed another knife and I ran out of the house. I ran and ran. I didn't know where I was going. We lived in an apartment at the time that was surrounded by homes. The road went into a half circle. I didn't know at the time. I ran in a half circle because I was going to run in someone's back yard and hide from him, but I heard dogs barking and I was afraid of dogs. I finally made it to a main highway, and this car was at the red light. I was bared feet and had on short shorts. Two guys were in the car. One of the guys said, "Hey baby, do you need a ride?" I was so tired I said, "Yea!!" The guy on the passenger side got out so I could get in the middle of them. I jumped in the middle and I put one knife on the right thigh and the other knife on my left thigh. "They were tall knives." They both looked and said, "Whoa!!! Baby, you must have been fighting with your man." I said, "Hell yea! And if you try something, I have a knife for you and a knife for you!" I said, "I bet you both be dickless when I finish with you!!" They said, "No baby, where you want to go?" I told them that I needed to get to a phone to call my husband's biological mother, who lived in Pompano Bch, Florida. She was a minister and a hairstylist. Her salon was attached to her house. I told her one day I would style hair too. She just smiled and said, "You must love it." She didn't know I was already pressing and curling my friend's hair before I left home. The two men took me to this much older couple home that they worked for, and the lady talked to me and told me that they were leaving for Tampa to pick their daughter up from the hospital. Her husband had beat her so bad and broke her ribs. I called my mother in law and she came all the way from Pompano, picked me up from the couple's house, and took me home. I asked her to please make sure my daughters were okay. She went in the house and she talked to her son and made sure my girls was okay. She called me inside and she talked to both of us and said we would never make it fighting and especially in front of the girls. She told us that she had been with her husband for 30 something years and he had never even raised a hand to hit her. I was amazed to hear that. How was that even possible? She talked to him about the letter and he confessed everything to me.

He promised me that it was over, and he wanted our marriage to work. I gave in because when things were good, they were great. He was a great dad to my girls and a great provider. We always went on family outings and vacations. One weekend we went to a park in Ft. Lauderdale where they had a giant swimming area. The middle of it was too deep for me and my girls. I began looking for my oldest daughter and my husband had my daughter out almost in the middle with him because she wanted to go a little further out. Myself and my youngest daughter was on the edge and when I looked back, I saw my husband just let his hands go from around my daughter and she fell in the water and was fighting to get up. I couldn't swim, but I was running in that water like I was on dry land. When he saw me running and screaming towards them, he grab her up and she was breathing very hard, and holding on to him for dear life, until I got there. I snatched my baby out of his arm and I started punching him saying, "You let her go!" He kept saying, "No, I didn't!" I punched him again and told him if he misses his children, he better go find them and don't try to kill mine. We left the park and when we got to the house I was going to leave. He fell on his knees crying and saying, how could I even think that he would do something like that to my child or any child. He begged me to believe him and he kept saying "I love you and those girls to death." I gave in and stayed there. We still had problems because I would forgive him, but I would never forget. So, I pretend a lot for the sake of having a home for my family. But the sex life was very dry. Late one night he wanted to have sex with me after a week of not having any from me. I was so hateful and still mad, I said, "No" and went to bed. He stayed in the living room on the floor looking at the television. I woke up around 1:30am. I could see him from the mirror on the dresser. He was in there playing with his penis. "What you would call jacking off." I was so upset with him because I thought about my daughters. I went in there and he almost jumped out of his skin. I started cursing at him, asking him what if my daughters had seen you? He went on about me not having sex with him. I went back to the letter and that started a physical fight. He hit me and I hit him back. He then grabbed me. My daughters woke up and came in the living room, and I told them to run next door to the neighbor's house to call the police! They went outside. I tried to get away, but he was holding me down choking me. Our dog jumped up and bit him on the arm. He let me go and hit our dog in the nose. My dog hollered and ran. That's when I got away and ran out the door. When I got pass the door I looked back and my daughters was plastered against the wall outside. I screamed for them to come with me. They ran and grabbed my hands and we ran together on the next street. The dog ran with us. We knocked on this couple's door and they let us in to use their phone to call his mother again. The couple was so scared, they said, "We don't want any trouble, but you can use the phone." I was so scared myself. She told my daughters to come in and have a seat. Here comes a knock at their door. The husband asked, "Who is it?" My husband asked him was it a woman and two children in there? The man said, "No." He told the man he was lying because my dog was on their porch. By that time, the man decided to call the police. Why did they send a policeman smaller than me! "The only thing big was his gun." When the police got there, it wasn't long after his mother arrived. This time she was mad, real mad, that Christian mad. She talked, and we prayed. She then took me and my daughters home with her. It was so peaceful there. I had a chance to watch her style her customer's hair. We stayed with her for a week. We went to church with her and that brought me back to praying and wanting to really get it right for my girls. We got back together, and we held each other and cried and put our family back together. We decided to buy a house, a nice house, huge yard with a fence around it. I moved up at my job because I stopped some thieves from stealing a cart full of meat. I became the Front end manager over the cashiers. Therefore, any new managers that was hired at the store, had to be trained by me. "They loved me." I helped my husband get a part time security job with one of the stores I used to work at. The manager who was over that store, I had trained him also. One day that manager called my new manager and asked him if I could have the next day off because I needed to come to his store and stop the deli manager and my husband from hanging out so much. She was a black, nice looking woman that was screwing one of the white boss's son. She was driving her nice Mercedes and stayed dressed up, even in the deli. I had worked with her before they opened that new store. We were not friends, but acquaintances. I got on the phone and he told me that they couldn't turn for each other. So, the next day I surprised my husband with a visit. Yep, soon as I walked in the store, they were walking down the aisle coming toward me smiling and talking to each other. "They both were in shock when they saw me." She came up and said, "Hey girl!" I was just telling your husband about the stealing going on in the deli. I said, "I've never seen you, or heard you telling any of the other security guards anything." "My husband walked off because he knew all hell was about to break loose." I had a towel in my hand with a knife wrapped in it. We walked back to the deli and she said "Listen, I don't want your husband." I said, "Okay well stay out of his face, everyday smiling and grinning!" Then she said, "Your husband can't give me nothing with a wife and two kids." I said, "That's right, no money or no honey bitch!" Then I started unwrapping my towel and I pointed the knife at her and said, "You don't know who you're messing with! I will take this knife and cut your head off and stick it in that deli window!" She said, "Wait a minute, I didn't mean any harm and I'm sorry if you think I did." Her workers was so happy to see her afraid of me because she treated them as if they were beneath her. My ex-manager came back there, and I hid the knife and we talked. He said he was just tired of looking at it and he knew I was a good wife and a hard worker. My husband and I talked about it and he said it was nothing.

 I said maybe I stopped something that was about to be something. After I wasn't pregnant the first time, we decided to try to have a baby. I had a good friend I met on the job. Her boyfriend and my husband became good friends. It was funny how we both was having symptoms of pregnancy. We both decided that we would go to the doctor together to get our tests done. Well we both got the same news, we were pregnant. The doctor told me I was about 16wks pregnant. My husband and I was so happy. The doctor scheduled me to have a sonogram. My husband wanted to go to the doctor with me, but his job was mandatory. I told him I would be fine. We kissed, and I went alone to the doctor. He was going all over my stomach and he just kept saying, I don't see no baby. He did another test and he said you have fibroids and tumors wrapped around your ovaries, that's why your stomach is this large and having symptoms of being pregnant. I asked him was he sure because the other doctor was so sure. He said yes, I am sure, and I am sorry. I had a huge decision to make. He said I needed to have a hysterectomy, and if I didn't, I would get uterus cancer maybe; 5, 10, or 15 years later, but I was definitely going to get it. I was so disappointed and hurt. How could all that happiness turn into so much sadness and pain. I knew for sure all the cheating and fighting would continue with my husband because he is stuck with a woman who can't even have children any more. I told my husband and my job that I needed to get away. My husband agreed that I should go back home to my mother and rest and think about what I needed to do for me. My daughters were still in school, so my husband said he would make sure they went. I was supposed to be gone a week, but during that time I decided I wasn't going back to him. His dad had finally got out of prison and he used to send for me and I wouldn't go, because my husband told me that when his dad saw me, that he said, "I should have been his woman." He didn't know that I knew what he had told my husband, but I wasn't going to entertain the thought. I called him this day to talk to my girls and he was fussing at me saying that his dad said that I had guys driving my car, and that he saw me with different men. Really! They were my cousins, nephew and brother. His dad didn't know them. My husband asked me when was I coming home? I told him I needed more time, especially after that conversation. The next morning, he took my girls to school and came to Belle Glade to make me come home. I was in my mom's house when I heard my niece say, "There go your husband." I looked up and there he was. I went outside to talk to him, but he just wasn't taking no for an answer. He hit me so hard that I fell to the ground. I told him, "I'm going to get you!" I ran in the house and got the longest knife my mom had. He ran and tried to jump in his car and lock the door. I pulled the handle before he could lock it. He was kicking and yelling. I went in with the knife. I was going to stabbed him in the chest, but he threw his arm up and the knife went in his arm. He finally got out the car because he was bigger than me. He tried to take the knife out of my hand. I was now fighting for my life. I threw the knife right down in front of two of my nieces that was standing there looking and neither of them picked it up. My husband went in front of them and picked the knife up and ran after me with it. I was running around and around his car. By then there were so many people out of their houses looking at us but not trying to stop us. Out of nowhere this blue van appeared and stopped. I heard this soft voice say, "Ya'll stop that." I tried to jump in the van with her. When I opened her door, my husband slammed the door shut and grabbed me by my neck with his left hand and had the knife in his right hand. When she called my husband's name, she said, "Don't kill your wife. Look at these people watching." She said, "I've known both of you since little kids. I know your parents." I looked at my husband and he had death in his eyes. My death! I begged him not to kill me. I told him that I would go home with him, just don't kill me. He looked at me and said, "Don't ever fuck with me again." I told him, "Bet it up!" (That meant never). He ran and jumped in his car and took off down the road. I called my friend girl and the police. I told my friend to go get my girls out of school and keep them until I got there. I told the police I would do what I needed to do when I returned from getting my daughters from Ft. Lauderdale. I left and got my girls. I moved in with my niece and a friend. My girls were with my mom. 2 days later I started hemorrhaging. I had big blood clots coming out of me. My mom called my husband and he decided to take me back to my doctor in Ft. Lauderdale, because he knew more about my situation. I think my husband got there in about 20 min. I hated it, but I felt as if I had no choice. He took me straight to the emergency room. The doctor told me I was having a miscarriage. I told him to please not mention that to my husband because there was no way I would ever want to be back with him. That was my secret between me and God. They took me in to surgery. They said I had lost too much blood. I needed to have a hysterectomy and a blood transfusion. They told my mom they were not sure if I was going to make it because I had lost so much blood. Of all people my dad came to see me. The visit was okay. My dad noticed that my arm was swollen. The IV had to be changed. Once my visit was over, they came to find another vein to put it in, but they had killed all of them. I heard them speaking about putting it in my foot. It was time to run away. They had already removed the old IV and left me alone. I put my clothes on and went to the first door. It said emergency exit only. They had chains on the door. I peeked around another corner and a nurse was at her desk, so I went another route and a security guard was there at another emergency exit. It was night. I don't know what would happen, but I was willing to take that chance. I went back to my room and changed my clothes and got back in the bed. Then the nurse came in and asked me, "Why are you so tired?" I told her I was trying to leave because they wanted to put an IV in my foot. She said don't worry we found the best person here to come find a vein in your arm. A few minutes later a short beautiful nurse walked right in there and had no problem finding a vein. (MY ANGEL). I was in there about 7 wks and my husband would visit me almost every day. The more he came, the sicker I got. Just the sight of him made me sick and the cologne he was wearing made it worse. I had a white nurse that took real good care of me and I told her everything about him. She despised him. I blamed him for everything. No more babies for the rest of my life. I was too young for this. I was 26 yrs old!! That meant every other man I may consider being with, must not want to have a child. WOW!!!!!!!!! I put in my mind that if they cheat on me and get someone else pregnant, I would have to hurt someone. I knew that would have to be the first thing that we'd discuss. I was getting better and they decided they were going to take the IV out of my arm and take me in the waiting area to see my daughters because I had not seen them in 2 weeks. I did okay for about 30 minutes, so they strolled me out there. I was so happy to see them, and they were happy to see me. I remember them running to me saying, "Mama!!!" I was out there for about 15 minutes and I started vomiting all over the place. They rushed me back to the bedroom and hooked the IV back into my arm. I was crying and so sad. I tried not to let it out, but I couldn't hold it. I was so sick that night. Then, I developed pneumonia and it was a battle staying alive. All I could think about was seeing my daughters again. I had to live for them. My day came when it was time for me to go home. My husband came and took me to his house that used to be home. My mother was with him. That night he begged me to have sex with him. I told him, "Hell no!!!!!!" He told me that he still loved me and wanted us to get back together. I had staples across my stomach and he wanted sex. That showed me how much he cared for me. I told my mom to call my brother to come and get us. We were supposed to stay a week. I left, and it took me a long time to heal physically but forever mentally. I started working at the Health Department as a cashier/bookkeeper. I loved my job. I felt high class; me off the streets and working a real decent job. Then came my worst nightmare! My husband quit his job and left the home and moved back to our home town. I knew that my freedom was over. He would send me flowers, and sometimes come by my job and take me to lunch. He even brought the family cat back with him. She was really my baby girl's cat. We started dating and my girls really loved him. They've always called him daddy. Finally, we moved back in together and he couldn't find a job. So, I told him about selling marijuana. I got him the hooked up and he started out small and worked his way up. Some of the women used to say, "Girl I saw your husband standing on the corner dressed nice while you're here working." I used to say, "I know." I wanted to say, "I hope you or somebody you know smoke weed." It wasn't long before business was booming with him. I continued working until they found out I had no high school diploma. My supervisor told me to take the GED test, and if I pass, I could keep my job. She was happy with my work performance. I took that test twice and that was the end of that job. I cried and cried. I started helping my husband bag the weed up and keep up with money. Soon he was buying pounds and we would have weekends away from the girls sometime and just smoke out and enjoy each other. We were the talk of the town; doing good, looking good and riding good. My Children were always very well dressed, and never from a thrift store. Don't have anything against them, I just made sure they didn't have too, because I wore enough for all of us. Like the saying goes, more money, more problems. The girls started chasing my husband, and the men started asking me to be with them. I was scared to death of him. The little girls wasn't scared of me enough not to sleep with him. To them he was new meat because when I met him, he was straight out of college and had a professional job. Now you are a street man, just like a regular drug dealer. I had created a big monster with a huge ego. After a while he got so big, he had guys working for him and still working his package. The entire time I was with him my baby brother was in prison. When I visited my brother, I told him little of what I was going through, but not everything because I didn't want him to worry about me. Someone else was telling him about all the fights my husband and I was having. It was this large family living there that was known for fighting, the same with my family. My husband started dating the younger sister. Two of the older sisters and I was pretty good friends, I would say. The younger crew was always saying little slick things and was so disrespectful to me. I tried to ignore them because my girls and I was being taken care of and I wasn't going to let some little girl stop that. My brother came home from prison and he was a street person and he saw my husband in an alley giving this girl some money. My brother didn't run and tell me this. I got dressed and went up the streets to join my husband. As we were walking down the sidewalk, his little girlfriend and three other people, one being an older female who knew me from way back, was sitting upstairs on a porch across the street from where we were walking, saying his name, and calling him; laughing as if I was not there. I told him, "You better straighten those hoes because you know when I get mad, I can't stop until I am finished.: I said to him, "Shit, I'm the wife, if anything I should be up there whipping her ass!!!" I told him that I don't have time for the foolishness!! He said, "I'm with you. I don't have anything to do with that." We had already had issues about this little girl, but nothing serious because we promised not to go by hear say because a lot of people did not want us together. I was so mad because they got louder with it, but the older one tried to stop them. I went home, I got my gun and I changed clothes and took my shoes off. I had 4 bullets for 4 hoes, as I called them. When I got back up there, they were gone. I walked from bar to bar looking for them with my gun in my hand. My brother from prison saw me mad and walking. He followed me. That's when he told me he saw my husband giving her money. He walked me home and on the way to my house we met my husband, and my brother went in his face and said, "Yea nigga, I been waiting to beat your ass just like you been fighting my sister!" He said, "And I saw you giving your little girlfriend some money." He was so mad with my brother that he wanted to fight him. I jumped in between them. He tried to tell me that my brother was lying to me, but I knew my brother wasn't lying because everyone knew including me about him and her. I just never caught them together. He was trying to reach for my brother, I put the gun to his head and I said to him, "If you hit my brother, I would kill you." He knew I meant every word I said. My brother didn't play about me and nor me about him. I told him, "My brother's eyes are just like my eyes seeing it." I convinced my brother to leave, and my husband and I went home.

Soon we moved across the street from my mom, and his dad and stepmother lived down the street from us. My sister lived down the walk way connected to the same building. My husband and I started talking about the same thing again, him cheating with this young girl. That was the talk of the streets. So, I confronted him again. He didn't want to hear it, so I left, I stayed with my mom. He would not let me take any clothes for myself or my children. He wanted me to come over every day to get what I needed. I started dating this married man that was big time in town and had so much money. He got me a room at the hotel to live there until I decided what I was going to do. He gave me a 45 pistol to protect myself, which I carried all the time. This man took such good care of me. I didn't care about going home with all the lies and cheating. At least I knew this man had a wife and had to go home. One day I was sitting in my mom house and my husband wouldn't give me our clothes. My daughter and my nephew went to the house and my husband had the young girl in the house with him. My daughter ran to me saying, "Momma, daddy got a lady in the house and she got on your night gown." I asked her, "Where is your auntie?" She said, "She is asleep." I know my sister would have tried to stop me. I automatically jumped up and grabbed my purse and went over to the house, all the time thinking, why not let me get me and my children clothes and whatever else belong to me. I knocked on the door and he told me to go away. I said, "No, I want my things out of here!" He opened the door and I could hear the shower running. I tried to go back there to the room where the shower was located, and he wouldn't let me. I said, "My clothes are back there and my children clothes." He pulled me back and told me "No!" He knocked me down on the floor.

I jumped up and hit him in the mouth. He tried to physically remove me out of the door. He tried to throw me out. My body got half way into the door and he slammed it on me. I jumped out and he shut the door and locked me out. I don't know why he let me in and he knows how I am. The door was designed with jalousie windows. After he did that he sat back on the couch as if he was a king, I took the gun out of my purse and turn it to knock the windows out and I pointed the gun through the window and looked at him and pulled the trigger. He screamed and fell on the floor. I could hear my sister call my name out loud. I ran through the alley and I saw my momma and her best friend across the street, standing there talking but trying to see what was going on. I ran across the street with the gun in my hand and I heard my mom say to my husband, "Don't you throw that rock!" I looked back and he was standing there with this big rock in his hand. I told him if he threw that rock and hit my momma that I would kill him. He threw it anyway but missed my mom. I pulled the trigger back and pointed it across the street at him and felt like my mind went into a dream state. My baby girl looked as if she was standing right next to him on roller skates. Then it looked like she wasn't there, but she was there more in my mind than not. I eased the trigger down and ran into my mom house. I opened the back door and threw the gun in a field of tall grass that was behind my mom's apartment. I ran in the closet, don't know why. I was shaking and scared. I knew I was going to jail. My daughter ran in the house screaming momma daddy got a shot gun and he's coming down the road. So, I told her to go back out there where my mom was. She left. I heard my mom call me and the sheriff was standing to the door. They sent 4 cops in two cars. One of the sheriffs grew up with me and my family. He asked me, "Where is the gun?" I said, "I don't have a gun." He said, "Carletha I know you have a gun because the hole in the wall is fresh and you missed his head by an inch." He said, "I can't help you if you don't give me the gun." I told him where I threw it. I asked him was he going to handcuff me, and he said, "No." So I got in the police car. His daddy was walking around the car saying out loud, "I'm going to get you, you tried to kill my son. I'm going get you." I looked at him and I screamed and said, "You're next!" During that time, I also was teaching a few Haitian men how to speak English. They were all looking at me sitting in that police car with a sad look on their faces. I did not cry. My mom and my sister was crying. They took me to the station and put me in a holding cell. The detective was yelling at me saying I was facing 15yrs at Laurie's women prison. I told him well I hate I missed. All the other polices knew me from visiting family members especially my brother. They knew every report of battery that I reported on my husband and restraining orders. My husband decided to come in my defense. He told them he did not want to press charges. I never saw him. They told me he came and left. One of the detectives that knew me walked in and looked at me in a surprise and asked, "What the hell are you doing in there?" I said, "I shot at my husband." He said, "Did you get him?" I said, "No!" Then he said, "I need to take you to the gun range." I laughed and said, "Okay." After about 3 to 4 hours they let me go home. Well I went back to the hotel I had. Once again, another ending of me and my husband. I had to try and focus on having fun, because I was reliving shooting at my husband over and over. The next day my sister and some friends came over and we had drinks and marijuana. We went down to the pool and our friend was teaching me how to swim. He was a good teacher, but when I thought I had learned I wanted to try on my own. I was in twelve feet of water. I took off and made it to the other side of the pool. I was so excited I wanted to go back. I took off and I got right in the center of the pool and got tired. I tried to stand up in twelve feet of water and I am only 5'3. I panicked. I went down and somehow, I made it back up. I could hear my sister screaming for help, saying, "My sister is drowning!" She ran to the edge of the pool but she thought about she couldn't swim either. I went down a second time.

I couldn't catch my breath. The water was over taking me. My eyes was going back into my head. When I went down for the third time my friend who was teaching me, came up with me in his arm and took me out of the water. I cursed him out because he told me that he would be there and let nothing happen to me. I don't think I should have nearly drown before he saved me. Never again did I even attempt to swim again. I should have known that I was still thinking about the shooting also. I lived there for about a month and my husband got his own room where his father was the rent man for that building. My daughter god mother had a trailer she wanted to rent so she asked me if I would like to rent it and I said, "Yes." It was a very nice two bedroom, three baths and a nice kitchen and huge living room space. I was so happy, and I was free and single again. My brother was back in prison again. So, I brought me a car so I could take my mom and myself to visit him. Before he went in this time, he had 3 children of his own. The lady he had two children from she used to go with my mom to see him with us most of the time also. My brother and her was planning on getting married when he came home. He was saying that he wanted to change his life and have a family to come home too. She would go out sometimes with me and my older sister to the club and they just have drinks and I loved to dance. Soon my brother's children mom started saying that she didn't want to go visit him anymore.

That was strange because to my knowing, they loved each other and was discussing marriage. Then I got the news that my sister bet a close friend that he couldn't date our brother finance, and as you know my sister lost the bet. He not only got her, they ended up moving in together. My brother was so hurt when he found out. We all knew him very well because he used to date my niece for years. Then she became pregnant from him. I knew my brother really wanted to give up on life. She was the only woman he ever loved enough to ask for her hand in marriage. He was devastated when she got pregnant. I don't know how, but he found out that the man did nothing but stayed drunk and beat on her. Somehow, he was told that the man was trying to touch his daughter inappropriately. He would ask me about it, but I had no idea what was happening in their house, and I wasn't trying to find out for him, because I knew how my brother would react.

I would never want to hurt him like that. I loved him too much to see him hurting the way he was hurting. He was losing his mind in prison. My brother was on work release and this day he decided to escape because he wanted to come and confront this man about what he had been hearing. He called me and told me that he had ran away from prison while they were out working in the fields. He wanted me to come pick him up. I was so afraid for him and myself, even though he was my brother. I would still be liable for his escape. I cried and begged him to turn himself in, because I didn't want them to find him and kill him. He promised me he would and that's just what he did. I was dating here and there and so was my husband. My men friends was so afraid of my husband. They wanted me but only if he didn't know. I could be sitting in the club with them and my husband would walk in and call me. My friend would say, "Hey your husband called you." I was so mad because here I am dating you, but every time my husband call me it's ok with you that I leave you to see what he want. Only because of how big and mean he looked. One day I met this tall dark and real handsome young man. Just gorgeous. He had that silky black skin with silky hair all over. His hair line was shaped like a v, front back and both sides. He was nineteen and I was twenty-five. He had just got out of prison. He was 6'2 and all muscles and wasn't afraid of anything, but not being with me. We used to have so much fun. We would go to the club and would turn it out. We both could dance, and we looked good together. We were the talk of the town, me once again. I didn't care what anyone thought. My mom hated my relationship with him. She used to always say, "Now you have three children." My daughters was crazy about him. They used to stand around the corner and just blush when he said something to them. I mean the whole town had a crush on him; women and gays. But he was mine, all mine. My husband came one night trying to fuss at me about a sweater my boyfriend had on that he said he bought. My boyfriend said to him, "I know you better get out of her face with that bull." They started arguing and I got in the middle of them. I did not want neither one of them to get in trouble, because it would have been a deadly match between these two. But I was very happy to know this young man was not afraid of him. I heard a rumor that my boyfriend was going around knocking men out he thought was disrespecting him or trying to have since on him, as he called it. I tried to tell him that no one was fighting and going home anymore. They were killing people. He said he wasn't afraid of no one. He moved in with us and my mom used to give me hell about him. It was hard for him to find a job. My mom used to say he think he's too cute to work. All they had was field work and there was no jobs available. His family loved me. He lived with his grandparents before he lived with me. He was his mom only child. I can say I helped him as much as I could until he found a job. My brother finally got him a job driving tractors with him. He was so happy to work and help me. My mom still didn't care she just didn't like him. Finally, the season was over, and his job ended. I lost the trailer and he moved back 12 miles from me with his grandparents.

Carletha Brown

We were so sad that we couldn't be together and had to be so far apart. Where he was living it seems as though when we talked to each other he had to defend himself from somebody. One man threaten him, he would shoot him. He said that he just sat there and laughed at him. I asked him why not just leave or if you ever need to run then you run. He said he's not running from no one. We were planning on joining a church and getting married one day. One day I was visiting him, and this young guy walked up to him and said what's up man, I wanted to kill him. I said, "What's going on?" He said, "That's the bitch that got me in trouble and I went to prison." He said, "I keep telling him to stay away from me." I said, "Wow!" I picked him up one morning and I brought him back with me and we got a hotel and he took his friend bike and rode it twelve miles home. The next evening, I was standing in front of the hottest record shop in town and he rode by with some friends and he saw me, and he told the guy to wait. He jumped out of the car and grabbed me and kissed me. He had got a haircut and had all the v shapes cut off. I asked him why because they were beautiful and natural. And I had got all my hair cut off to get a jerri curl. We were both bald and shock. He told the guy to circle the block again, and he repeated this for 7 times. Just kept kissing me and telling me how much he loved me. And I loved him. The next day I was braiding my niece hair and his best friend walked in the living room where I was, and I said, "Where my baby, is he with you?" And he said, "He's dead." I looked at him and I said, "What?" He said, "That's why I'm here. I thought you knew." He said, "His mom and family are at the hospital." Twelve miles away I jumped up and my niece and I drove so fast to get there. When I got there, I saw his momma running away from the hospital screaming, "Lord my baby, my only child, Lord my baby dead!!" I knew it was true. As I walked in the hospital and his grandfather told me he was just getting ready to come tell me as soon as he left the hospital. He asked me if I wanted to see him, I just laid on him and cried. How could this strong young man be dead? I had a lot of his shirts and tank tops that he wore, and I could smell his body all over them. I can't even explain the pain and grief I went through. My mom came to me and said, "I didn't like him, but I never wanted him to die." But she still never held me. The newspaper read man gets killed over bicycle. I heard that he was at the high school gym playing ball and the same young man who he said sent him to prison got the bike and left with it. When he got ready to leave it was gone and 10 min into his waiting, the guy was riding on it. They said they began arguing and my man beat the mess out of him. They said my man was home sitting on his grandparent porch and the guy came shooting at him. He jumped up and started running from him and the bullets. He ran until one of the bullets hit him in the back and the bullet burst his heart open. He fell on the church yard. His granddad say he went up there and called his name and he looked at him and fell dead. By now my husband had move a woman in with him and told me how sorry he was to hear about his death. I got my own apartment and I start hanging out in West Palm Beach partying and back to snorting cocaine and smoking weed. I was still in shock, hurt, and wanting to ask, "Why Lord?" He never tried to hurt me nor my kids. He was hot headed but not with me. My mom had my daughters while I was trying to figure things out. I was right back where I started. My husband had finally moved on but still wanted me in the picture. He was too far into his relationship to just dump her for me. They were a couple and they looked good together just like we did. Yes, I was very jealous, but I was not going to be number two, so my daughter Godmother who was also my mom best friend offered to let me rent her house she had in West Palm. By me visiting prior to moving there I already had connections to do what I knew best.

Chapter 8

NEW CITY FOR ME

My friend and another sister that lived in West Palm moved in the house with me. The house was huge and had a big fence around it. I left my daughters with my mom until I got back on my feet. I never let them know what I was doing. All they knew is that mom always had a lot of money, and my mom and my daughters never wanted for nothing. I furnished my house with what people that were smoking crack brought to me, if it was nice. I've always had beautiful homes and always kept them very clean. I met a Jamaican man that was huge into dealing drugs, he was as big as they could get. He drove a Jaguar, looking back, that was like driving a Rolls Royce. He was handling kilos. He didn't know anything about cooking cocaine until I showed him, but he only did it for me to sell and make my money. I thought I had died and went to heaven, I never had to worry about being poor ever again. Soon he started asking me to ride with him, me not knowing where I was going, went with him to deliver keys of cocaine to doctors and lawyers. I was amazed at that. They'd always asked him if they could have me too. I was always a sharp dresser, I would say, "Oh no it's not that kind of party." They would say, "But you are so pretty." Then he would say, "Thank you but she belongs to me only." I was so scared and nervous about riding with him doing that. He was so good to me that I was afraid to say I didn't want any part of that. I finally built up my nerves to tell him I didn't like him taking me with him delivering drugs, I knew I was not built for that. Every time he would spend the night with me the police would always come to his car. I thought they always wondered what a Jag was doing parked in my neighborhood. I started feeling so bad about what I was doing to my own people. I wanted a way out but didn't know how. There was a mother and two daughters that was hooked so bad on crack they used to ask for the crumbs from cutting the cocaine. The daughters were adults and their mom was in her 50's. The mother would even write me notes with a face that she called aping. I was so hurt because I thought of my daughters. There were college students trying to sell me their nice cars and clothes. I prayed and prayed for God to show me a way out. This was too big for a country girl who thought she knew how to handle big time. One day he called me and told me he had a friend from the Bahamas there picking up two kilos of cocaine from him and he wanted me to fly to the Bahamas to pick up the money. I was scared to death. I had never been on a plane and all I thought about was this man could kill me. Why didn't he already have his drugs, I thought to myself. I told my older sister who had just move to town and saw how I was living how nervous I was about going. She said if you don't want to do it, I will. All she thought about was he said he would get me a hotel and I can go shopping. I told her no!! I will go before I let you go. I really prayed for God to intervene in this mess I had gotten myself into. The day I was supposed to leave he called me and told me that the man called him and said, "I'm not giving you shit, I have my drugs and you can't leave the country." I was so happy. I fell on my knees and thanked God for his protection. After that my friend went to prison and from what I heard he got life. I wasn't happy about that because he was a very sweet person. After that I met a guy from Miami. I was with some friends walking the strip in the ghetto, or hood part of town, where everyone who was somebody, and drugs addicts were hanging out. This guy pulls up in a Mercedes and jumped out into my face and said, "Get the hell from up here! You don't belong up here!" I had never seen him before in my life. I told him to get out of my face, he said, "I'm not playing with you. This is no place for you." So, I left with my friends and went home. We became the best of friends. He became my big brother and daughter's uncle. By then I had put in for a house on housing because I wanted my daughters with me.

I missed them like crazy. My housing came through. I signed up for cosmetology school, and my sister moved to Ga. My best friend got her own place on housing also. We promised each other that we would never try crack cocaine because we saw the affect it had on everybody else who was using it. I was so happy to be going to school, so I went to get my girls and my mom didn't want them to leave. I told her I needed my girls with me. She said she believe she would have a heart attack if I took them, and I told her I would have one if I didn't take them. I got my girls and I got a job working at Morrison Cafeteria. I was so happy. My drugs selling days were gone. And my social worker told me that she had to hide my files, so I could continue to go to school for cosmetology. She said she was happy that I decided to go. I thank her a million times because when I started working she became one of my customers. Then I found out that my oldest daughter was pregnant, she was 15 and the father said he couldn't take care of a baby because he was still in school. I told my daughter if she wanted to keep her baby, I would try my best to help her take care of it. I told her I would always be pro choice, because I never wanted either of my daughters to ever say that I made them have a baby or I made them have an abortion. They would have to make that decision, not me. And I would never help them financially for an abortion. So, her boyfriend didn't want any part of her pregnancy. Later into her pregnancy she met a young man that seem like he adored her. He was telling everyone that my daughter was pregnant with his baby. He was selling drugs and started buying her all these clothes and jewelry. He brought her a car and she couldn't even drive. My youngest daughter used to drive her car for her. Only thing when she had her baby, she looked identical to her biological father. "He was so angry." Then he started getting very jealous of her being with her baby. He began beating on my daughter. She told me that she didn't like him. She only liked what he did for her. She also said when he started snorting cocaine that's when he became violent with her. He convinced her to move in with him and his mom, but I kept her baby because I was afraid of what he may do to her. You know where there's housing there is drugs and drug dealers. One day the school was looking for my daughter because she was always an honor roll student. I went to talk to them, she had missed so many days living with him. I was at work one day and she called me crying saying her jaw might be broke. I was so angry with him because I didn't like him at all hitting on my child. I went to get her and took her to the hospital. "I wanted to kill him." I went through that and I wasn't going to sit by and watch my daughters go through the same thing. That evening he drove through the neighborhood and someone told me he had a gun, and I told them to get out the way because I had one too. And we were going to be two shooting mother fr's in this alley tonight if he continues driving through. Then she met someone that ran him off and she started dating him because he wasn't afraid of her ex-boyfriend. My newly found brother stayed in my life coming by every now and then to make sure we were okay. Finally, my mom moved to West Palm Beach, not far from me in an apartment. My brother and his kids and their mom moved in with her. I was happy. When I went out of town she could watch my daughters for me. I use to ride to Miami with my friend some weekends and we would sit all night snorting with different friends of his. Sometimes it felt like my heart was going to jump out of my chest. I would come back home and try to function for my children and my schooling. I met some of his friends that were working with him selling drugs, they started having problems with guys from my home town. They had a bad shoot out one day, two different towns fighting over turf. One day they caught one of his friends coming out of a store and shot him in the back and they brought him to my house. The guy had a hole so huge in his back, I didn't know what to do. I told them to take him to the hospital and he didn't want to go. I called my friend and told him and he came there immediately. He looked at his back and scream, "Got Damn man it's bad!" He said, "Man it's really bad!" The guy looked in the mirror and fainted. They rushed him to the hospital. He lived. Then I heard there was a retaliation on my home town boys. Then one night my friend –big bro, was riding and was caught at the red light and was shot 6 times. My nephew came and told me what happen. It was bad and all I could do was scream and cry and pray that God spared his life. I had to wait to go to see him because his baby momma thought we were seeing each other. He tricked her to go buy him something from the store, so I could come see him. He was so messed up. One of the bullets hit his intestines and they told him he had to wear a bag on his side for a few months. He told me that if he was told he had to always wear it he would kill himself. He said, if it wasn't for him being so high on the cocaine he would have died. He said that's what the doctor told him. I worked and continued school while he was in the hospital. I met my second husband at Morrison, he was one of the chefs in the kitchen. We started dating and things were going great. He told me about his two sons who lived in Ga. with his mom. He said when he got a divorce the mother told him to take them with him. He had his own apartment and I was a project girl. We dated for a few months then he took me to meet his mom and his sons. I felt special and I was trying to change my surroundings. Only I was still smoking weed, snorting, and smoking cigarettes. He didn't know I was doing anything but cigarettes, and he hated it. So, I made sure when we were with each other I didn't smoke around him, I couldn't wait for him to leave so I could get into my zone. His mom was a cigarette smoker too, only she smoked Winston. At first, I was ashamed to tell her, but I told her he didn't want me smoke and she said child smoke this before he gets back. I pulled on that strong cigarette and got drunk, "but I was in cigarette heaven." We sat there and laughed and became good friends. When we got back from Georgia, I continue to date him, and he decided he wanted to marry me. In school I was one of the top hairstylists. When I first started, I was hanging with the wrong crowd. I had to get it together because that was my other love. I finished school early. My instructor told me I was ready at 1000 hours. which normally takes 1200 hours to complete. My man used to come see me every day before he went home from work then things change, he slowed down. I would go back to Belle Glade to hang out with some of my friends and niece and would let my girls visit my ex husband and his new woman. They liked her, besides that they still called him dad. Soon he started fighting her and she moved out. He started snorting cocaine and selling crack on the streets. He was still dressing nice and keeping himself up. A month later I took my girls back to visit and he looked like he had lost a lot of weight. But it wasn't noticeable, but I knew. One of my friends told me that he had been hanging out late and sometimes all night with my niece getting high. She said, "Carletha I believe they are sleeping together." Yes, the one who lived with my baby father, she couldn't stand my husband when we were together. My friend said sometimes he would be so high he would take off his shirt and be racing with the

A Cry for Help

young boys. When I went to visit my home town, he would always give me money and weed. I would give the weed away, or only smoke when I went there on weekends. I asked him what was wrong with him and he said he went to the doctor and he said he had a touch of pneumonia. The first thing I thought about was HIV. We were in the club and he asked me was I staying overnight, and I told him yes. So, he asked me if I needed a hotel. By that time my niece walked up and said yea we need somewhere to stay; her not knowing what our friend had told me. He smiled and said, "I'll get you a room," I said, "No, I'm engaged to be married." And she said, "I will stay the night with you." So, I said, "Okay sense she said she would stay." On the way there she told me that she told my ex husband that she would get me to the room if he would give her some cocaine powder. I told her I bet he beat you back up the street!!! She said, "If he start kissing them thighs, you'll open up." I asked if she wanted to bet some money on that. I said, "He knows me better than you, I was married to this man." We got to the room and he is already there, we walk in and she say to him, "Give me my shit." Then she said bye and left. We sat down and talked. I told him I was in love with my soon to be husband. He told me that all he can say is if he treats me right, he have his self a good woman. I told him I will always love him, but I am not in love with him anymore, then he left. The next time I saw him he went from 250lbs to 100lbs. I knew then what was wrong with him. There were humors that he had HIV and now he had full blown AIDS. "Look at GOD." My brother, who played basketball and my ex-husband became close friends during the years and especially since we had divorced, I heard they used to double date. He kept me informed about his health because he was living with another young girl and had a baby boy by another one. My brother told me that he couldn't walk anymore after the last time I saw him, and the young girl was leaving him home alone. So, I called his biological mom in Pompano to please go to Belle Glade and get him to a hospital. Then I called his older brother and asked him also. I was so worried about him, but I couldn't do anything to help because his girlfriend felt threaten by me. Well they finally got him to a hospital, and he had just what I thought. I told my future husband all about what was going on with him and I needed to take my daughters to see him. When we got there, he was happy to see them, then his girlfriend came in with all that drama about me being there. I left because he didn't need to hear all that mess. She said something smart to me and I called her a bitch. I went down to the parking area and I flatten one of the tires on her car. My girls told me not to fight her because she could possibly be sick too. She went and told his daddy that I flatten all 4 tires and I called her a bitch. He soon died, and his father said he didn't want me to his funeral, but my girls could come. I was sad for him, but my daughters were hurt because they weren't going to his funeral either. I thank God for placing me in another man's life and was engaged to someone I loved, and that one night I didn't give in to lust. I could have gotten caught up in that web of HIV. Even though I was not dealing with him sexually for a long time I still decided to get tested. The hard part is not knowing but the hardest part is waiting on the results. All the people he was dealing with started dying or drying up one by one after he died. After that happen, I didn't visit as much as I used to.

A different time I was riding back one day with my niece, she was driving as we were coming down the highway. We saw some prisoners working on the road. We had to come to a complete stop and my niece threw her hand up and said, "This mother is fixing to hit us!" Before I could turn around a big cement truck hit us from behind and knocked us down in a dry ditch and on the other side was a lake full of alligators. The car turned all the way around going down the hill and I saw the truck hit the prisoner that was holding the sign for us to stop. Then the truck came down the hill and hit us again, the truck flipped over, and the guy fell from under the truck. We had cement and glass all in our hair and all the windows were shattered. All the prisoners ran to the car and I was trying to get out of the car because I didn't want the car to blow up. One of the prisoners said, "Get out, get out," So I stood up and another said, "No, no sit down, sit down." Soon there were state troopers and ambulances everywhere. They put me on this hard board and a neck brace and rushed us to the hospital. They released me that day and gave me muscle relaxers for my back. My back and neck were killing me, I had to go see a chiropractor. In the meantime, my niece called an attorney she saw on tv and the investigator called me. I didn't know anything about the law. The investigator told me since my niece called for them that I had to take them too. They played us like a yoyo, well maybe just me because she settled right then and there. She said she didn't have time to be going back and forth to no doctors. I was hurting, my family thought I was pretending to be hurt, but I didn't care. They finally settled and gave us a little money and the first thing I did was go buy me a car. My man was still missing in action at times and sometimes didn't even answer his phone. We were going on almost two years, planning a wedding. I pass my test and started working in a salon as a shampoo girl. It was hard with my back hurting, but I was always able to tolerate a lot of pain. I was ready for a big change for me and my family. I was also ready to get from living right next to the train tracks. That was so annoying. I had to find out what was going on with him. I went to buy something to eat and my mind and my car took me to his apartment. When I got there and parked the car, I looked next door at him and he was coming out of another apartment putting on his shirt. But all of them looked alike so I got confused and thought I was at the wrong house. But he came over to his place and met me and we went in his house, I asked him who's house he just walked out of. He said that's the lady I told you who was keeping the boys during the summer when they visited. So, I said oh okay then let me go introduce myself to her because we're getting married. I need to tell her thanks. He said, "No!!" I said calmly, "I'll be right back." I went over there, and I knocked on the door. The young lady came to the door and opened it. I was shocked because it was a lady who hair I did previously. Her mother was there with her. I said "Hello, he told me you were the baby sitter." She said, "No," I said, "No?" Her mother screamed, "You don't owe her no dam explanation." F- her, she said, "No ma, we need to talk." I didn't understand why her mom was so upset with me. I said, "We been together for two years," and she said, "I been with him for a year." "My eyes bucked." I said, "Well, we are planning a wedding in Feb," Here it is Dec." She said, "Really?" She said, "The way I found out about you was one day you were doing my hair and I heard you talking about your man wife divorced him and left their two sons with him and they lived in Ga with his mom." She said, "That night I confronted him about you, and he showed me a picture of you and him at a club and I knew it was you." I said, "Well for the last four months he has been coming pretty regularly to my house." She said, "Yea because I wouldn't let him in mine." I was totally caught off guard, I left and went home. I cried all night and all the next day. My best friend came over and she called my big bro and he came and took both of us to Miami and got a hotel. We went to a friend of his house and snorted cocaine for about two hours and went to the hotel and stayed all night playing cards and snorting. My eyes were so swollen from crying so much. I looked in the mirror I didn't recognize who I was. My bro asked me to let him kill him, I said, "No! There is no way I could live the rest of life knowing you killed him." I told him I would get over it one day and he is not worth it! He said man look at you he hurt you and you been good to that mother, he said, "You even stopped hanging out with me for his stank ass." He was mad and serious, but I had to calm him down. I didn't know what to do about the wedding. His aunt was making the dresses for my bride's maid and most of everything was being taking care of by the coordinator. He kept coming to my house begging and pleading with me. He said, "When we got married, we would move into a place together and he was sorry." He said, "My family love you and I love you and your family, please let's do this." "I gave in."

Chapter 9

HUSBAND # TWO

On that Feb we had one of the biggest weddings I could ever dream of and he was an hour late. I did ask my dad to give me away. At the last minute he told me he didn't have the money to get his tux, so I had to pay for that. I was so angry with him. I dressed my mom from head to toe with a smile. Because I knew I loved my mom and my mom loved my daughter. My husband paid for our wedding. He also catered the food himself. My only sister from my mom told me that if she wasn't my matron of honor that she wasn't coming to my wedding. I had to tell my friend that it would just be two matrons of honor. The wedding turned out beautiful. The next month they came to repo my husband's nice car. I couldn't understand that. How do you have a huge wedding and lose your car? "I guess I was worth it after the damage he did." During this time my dad was dating a mom and her daughter. He had the mom living in the house with him and made the shed in the back of the house for the daughter's bedroom. The daughter got sick. My dad took advantage of another young girl. He was sleeping with them both, and because she was young, and my brother was young he accused my brother of trying to sleep with the her. He didn't ever want my brother around her. The daughter got pregnant from him and I heard that's how the mom found out. I was so disappointed and ashamed of what he had done. The mother left my dad and he continued his life with the daughter. It was time to focus on my own family. At eighteen years of age, my daughter was pregnant with her second child. My husband and I still had her first child living with us. She was living with her baby father at this time. He was also taking good care of her, but I heard about him hitting on her. Sometimes she would tell me things but would never leave him. She had another baby girl. I would fuss at him about putting his hands on my daughter and he would just look at me but never disrespect me like the last one tried. "Only he sold drugs also." I really had no problem with that because I used to do it too. So, who was I to judge him at that time in my life, but they knew I wasn't afraid of no one and nothing. Just keep your hands of my child. I just really had to change for my family's sake.

Well I tried to make it work with my husband, but he was a sneaky cheater. All of his dirty work was done on the job. I heard one time he had a girl in the cooler making out. He changed jobs and started working for this catering company and doing his own catering on the side. I continued working in the salon as a shampoo person until one day the owner of the salon got so busy. He asked me to finish the young lady hair, and he was amazed that I knew how to style hair. He had a few hair, nail and fashion shows that I helped with and models, and sometimes I modeled for him. I loved showing my talent and modeling. We moved into another house and my husband car was in the shop and this young lady was bringing him home and they would sit in the yard talking. I went out there and told her the next time she came here with my husband in her car I was going to beat the shit out of her. His cousin had already called me and told me that the girl told her she was sleeping with him. I told her, "I don't care if it's raining, or snowing let him walk!" she was a hot mess, ugly mess. I had to nip that in the bud before I end up in prison.

I used to drive sometimes to Georgia to pick his boys up alone, because he couldn't get off from work. When I got back, I got some woman calling my house cursing me out. I asked him who he gave the number to and he would say nobody. Then here come the momma that gave her boys away thinking that she could to come to my house when she gets ready, I'm the one doing all the driving to get them and sometimes take them back. She made so many promises to those boys that she never kept. I would have to make it up to them. I really loved those boys and they loved me. It was hard to see them hurting from her lies. I told her don't come to my house anymore and she said, "I don't want your husband I had him." So, I told her to act like it, every year I'm driving that road to pick up their boys and sometimes taking them back to Ga; "I told her I would dig a hole in my yard and bury her ass in it." She left. At the same time, I'm hearing that my oldest daughter is being beat on by her second baby father again. Yep like I said he was just as worst as the first one. He kicked her in the stomach while she was carrying his baby. I went off on his behind! But he would still just look at me and say nothing. That day I was ready to give him a good fight or kill him. They broke up for a while and she went back to him. She called me one day I was working at another salon and the same baby father had her baby outside at my house threaten to put the baby in the trunk of his car if she didn't come out my house. She called me screaming and crying telling me this. I left work so fast. And when I got there, he was standing there with their baby in his hand with the trunk open. I walked right up to him and took the baby out of his hand and said, "Give me my damn grandbaby!" I took the baby in the house to my daughter. I told her I wish he would say something I will fight his little skinny ass. He didn't say a word. He got in his car and left. I went to bed one night and I dreamed that my husband was at work and I walked in and he was lying back in a woman lap. The next day I walked into his job and this girl was standing in a window where they send the food out and she was talking to someone at the window. Everyone in there just stopped working and their eyes bucked when they saw me. When I walked to the window it was my husband. He was grinning from ear to ear. Some of the workers went up to her whispering in her ear. I heard her screamed SO!!!!!!! She looked at me crazy and I looked at her crazy. I asked him what the hell is going on. He always said, "It's nothing." And then gave me a peck on the lips. Later a friend of a friend told me she screamed So because they were telling her, that's his wife! I found out that she was the young lady calling my house cursing me and my youngest daughter out because she thought my daughter was me. My oldest daughter went to Adult Ed and got her high school diploma, because she scored so high on the test. They had a graduation for them at the auditorium and the same girl on his job graduated too. After the ceremony we were walking to the car and she looked at my husband and smiled and he smiled back.

It took all I had not to slap his lips off. I was so happy for my daughter and didn't want to ruin her day. At the same time, I got a letter from my brother telling me that someone hit him the back of the head with a weight bar and he wasn't feeling good, and if anything happens to him, to check into it. After the boy's summer vacation, my mom and I drove them back to Ga; because on our way up we could stop to see my sister in Ga and on the way back we could stop to see my brother. On our way back, we went to the prison called Radford, which is a place where murders get sent. He is the one who got attacked and hit in the back of his head. We went to see my brother and as the guard was searching me, she said, "Your brother is so sick, please check on him because they don't care nothing about these inmates." She said, "He is really sick!" My heart dropped. When we got in there, I could see him walking towards us staggering a little. He was so weak. As we were talking to him it was as if he was in a daze. I was so hurt because before this time my brother got locked up, he was smoking crack, dealing and hanging around the wrong crowd. He never got over losing his family, and when he did come home, she wouldn't let him see his children.

Before he got locked up my mom asked me to give him money so that he could leave town, so I did. The next day I come home he was standing on my porch with two white guys and they all were high. He took the money and brought drugs so when he got locked up, I told him I was tired of trying to help him and he didn't want to help himself. I was so hurt to see him like that, all I could do was cry. I took a picture with him at the prison and I had to hold him up. On the way home I cried like a baby while I was driving. My mom was trying to talk to me, but I was so hurt. When I made it home, I called Tallahassee. I called everyone I could think of to get my brother to a doctor. I called the prison and talked to the head man there, and the next day they transferred him back to Lake butler. They called me and told me that he had slipped into a coma. They told me they kept saying my name and he was trying to wake up. They rushed him to Jacksonville Memorial Hospital. I was going back and forth to Jacksonville every chance I got. They always had guards by his room. I came back, and I told my husband I needed to be with my brother, and he asked how he was going to get to work. I told him do what he knows best. Have one of his girlfriends to help him, he was cheating anyway. He didn't want me to go. I didn't care that was my brother, so I left and moved to Ga, to be closer to my brother in Jacksonville. I went every other day to visit him. I even drove back to Belle Glade and got his children hoping if he just heard their voices he would wake up. The doctors kept saying he was on a lot of medicine and that's why he was out. So, I asked them to lower the medicine and let us call his name because he was fighting to wake up. My brother stayed in a coma for a long time and they decided that if someone in the family was physically able to take care of my brother that they would release him in their custody. The doctor said that his brain cells were deteriorating from the hit in his head. My older sister was not able, and they say my mom was not able, so I asked what about me. They said yes, all I needed was for my mom and dad to sign a paper releasing him to me. My dad had not made it up there the whole time to see my brother. I was already upset with him. Two days went by and my dad called me and said he was waiting on his car to be fixed. I went ahead and got an apartment. My oldest daughter and her two kids moved with me. While I was in Georgia, I received a phone call saying that my best friend was smoking crack. The one that we promise me that we would never try it. She got hooked up with this Jamaican man that was selling it and they wanted to try it with sex. She had two sons. The youngest was my godson. Finally, her man got busted and she had to end up in Belle Glade with her sister. The family of her oldest son took him from her. The next week I called my dad and I said I want to know, when are you coming? I want to bring my brother home with me. He said something about a toothache. I was very angry with him. Sometimes when I really get stressed out, I would go to a hotel to get some rest or just meditate. This evening I woke up from crying and I was so tired. I was in a hotel and I called my dad and I said, "Daddy I'm still waiting," and he said to me, "Oh he dead, Bobby is dead." I just could catch my breath. He said, "Yea they called me this morning and told me he had died." I said, "I was waiting on you! all this long time I been waiting on you!!" I hung up the phone and I screamed, hollered, cried, and tried to pray. My baby was gone, my brother! I threw things around in the room because he had to die alone without his family being with him. I went back home to be with my mom because I knew this would really hurt her. She did try her best to take care of him, but when my brother and I turned eighteen my mom cashed in our insurance policies. Now we are wondering how we were going to get him home and how we were going to bury him. My dad came to Belle Glade when we had to talk to the funeral director about money and arrangements. The mortician said that the prison had on my brother's death certificate that he died from HIV. The mortician said, "This was no way, a body with HIV." They were saying it was like eighteen hundred dollars to bring him home from Jacksonville to West Palm Beach Air Port. My dad had the nerve to ask me if I could get a station wagon car and drive him back. I thought that was the lowest of the lowest. I asked him how in the world he thought I could drive knowing that my baby brother was in the back dead. I told him to do it. "I felt like slapping his false teeth out his mouth!" He helped my mom make all the arrangements and told us he was going so he could get some money to help pay for everything. We never saw him again before then or after the funeral. I went around town asking for donations to help, but it wasn't nearly enough. God showed up and my mom's best friend's husband came to my mom and told her that he would loan her the money, and just pay him as she could. On the day of the funeral the mortician was lining the family up and he called my dad name and he wasn't anywhere to be found. Months later he said my younger brother had a baseball game, the son he raised. I was so mad at him. How could you embarrass my mom and family like that? He wouldn't even answer his phone. My ex came to be with me. I prayed for my strength because I did not want him to touch me, because he didn't want me to go and see about my brother. I had so much hatred inside of me. He never had a chance in life. He had no education or no real love from anyone but me and my mom. I heard that my matron of honor went to my house while I was away with nothing on but a trench coat and a pair of high heels, and my husband slept with her. I heard my brother's girlfriend of about 12 years then, went there asking for money because she was hooked on cocaine and it has always been a question of did, they sleep together also. I left and remained in Georgia. Later, my mom wanted to come to Georgia, so me and my sister was talking. She told me that she thought that my mom should live with me because my mom wasn't that clean, and she like to throw her meat in the freezer bare and have grease everywhere. We both kind of laughed about it because it was true. I said, "She wants to live with you, not me." I told my daughter to watch how they both get together and gain up on me for nothing. My daughter thought all those years of telling her how my sister and mother felt about me was a myth of mine. As soon as my mom got there all she started doing was criticizing me. She and my sister became best friends. I felt like a loner most of the time. My youngest daughter was supposed to be living with her father in Pahokee and I heard she had left and was living with my niece in Belle Glade. She was seventeen, almost eighteen. She told me she wanted to be with her dad. Instead she left him and went to live with her. I was highly upset because I knew what type of life style she would have being there and with her. I was told that she had my daughter asking men for money to pay her end of the bills in order to live with her. I got a phone call that I needed to come and get her. My nephew was headed there, so I asked him to bring her back. Now I had both of my girls and my mom with me in Georgia. My nephew and my daughter helped me get my own salon up there because every salon I went in and presented my work they either looked scared or said no. My sister told me, you can't just come up here and open a salon and think you're going to make it. She said, "These people already have their own beautician up here." I found a salon that was empty and opened it and my nephew wife was my receptionist. I started a commercial on TV on Sunday gospel. I tell you people was coming from everywhere. Even some of the beauticians that told me no came to me.

 I kept waiting on my license to come from Georgia's State board instead I received a letter saying that Georgia requirements was different than Florida. They wanted me to go back to school and get 500 more hours and the nearest school was twenty-eight miles away. I had been licensed eight years. I was not trying to make Georgia my home. I really was ready to leave. I was miserable. My ex-husband came through when he went to visit his mom and boys and asked me to please come back home with him. After not being happy there and I hated the cold weather, I came home not even wanting to be back with him. I just needed to get back to Florida and retain my mental stability. I came back home and was not happy with him. It had been too much happening while I was gone and when I was gone. I looked at him I thought about him not wanting me to take care of my brother.

Carletha Brown

My niece came by and told me about my friend on drugs again. I went to find her, and she was so small. It was a hundred degrees outside, and she had on a wool hoody on her head and had a blanket on top of her. Her finger nails were so dirty. She always loved to keep her hair and nails clean. She was so mad that someone told me that she was smoking crack. She was cursing and talking crazy. But she would not get up off that couch so that I could really see her. I saw enough to know she was a crack head. After I left, two weeks later she called me and asked me if she could come live with me and my husband. I told her, "No way." I said, "The only place I would take you is to a rehab center and get you some help." She said, "She didn't need any help." Me not knowing she had stabbed her new boyfriend who was also selling crack and smoking. "He died." She caught a ride with a truck driver with her youngest son. She went to Georgia where my family was living. On the way there she told the truck driver what happen. The truck driver called the police after he dropped her off and told them where she was. The Detectives went up there with the help of the Georgia police. They went in my niece house with guns out everywhere and got her. None of my family up there knew what happen. They were going to put her son in a foster home in Atlanta. I just couldn't see that happening and he was my godson. My husband didn't want me to get him we had a big argument about that. So, I just waited to see what was going to happen. They brought her back to Florida and locked her up in the women's stockade. I went to visit her. When she came out you could count her ribs. We just held each other and cried. I said look where you are, we promised each other. She cried and said he kept telling me it was good with sex and to try it and I did. Then the new boyfriend she explained that they were arguing about crack in the hallway and it was dark. She thought she had cut him, not stabbed him. She asked me to please get her son, and I promised her that I would try. The judge gave her seven years. My husband started telling me to get out of the house and go to my home town to visit my family. I told him, "You better leave me in the house while I'm here," but he insisted on me going. He said, "Sometimes when I come home, I don't know who I'm going to meet at the door." Sometimes you're happy when I come home and sometimes you act like you hate my guts. On weekends I would call my niece to come pick me up. I

A Cry for Help

started going to the club and this night it was this group called La-Wav and they sounded just like Boys To Men. They were awesome. The shortest guy, but the loudest called me on stage and sat me in a chair and sang Baby Hold On To Me. He got down on one knee and kept singing and walked over to the mirror and then he turned upside down on the mirror and started rolling his hips. In my mind, I was saying, if he can do that on the mirror, I can imagine what he can do in bed. I was hooked. I started going every weekend. Soon my husband was getting upset. I told him I asked you not to push me out of the house and I told him I'm not happy here and I'm leaving you.

Chapter 10
A CHANGE IS COMING

I left with a brown bag and started living with my second oldest brother. I was doing hair at his house to make my money. I would help him with food and keeping the house clean. He helped me out a lot whenever I needed him too. I started seeing that short man on a regular. Everybody kept saying how are you going to come here and take that woman husband. I had no idea what they were talking about. He was still living with his parents, not a wife. Soon my mom came home from Georgia and my youngest daughter. We were all living with my brother in his small apartment. I was having a ball doing hair and going out hanging with the group. My youngest daughter started dating one of the other singers in the group without me knowing right away. So we both traveled with them to different clubs or just met them there. My oldest daughter came from Georgia and she was pregnant with her third child. She had attended college up there and was doing great in school. She was upset if she made a B. I saved up enough money to get a nice apartment, 3 bed rooms, 2 baths. So, my two daughters and I, my grandchildren, and they finally gave me my godson, and we all moved in together. I went and rented a living room suite and we manage with sleeping on the carpet. One day my new man came to the house and he saw that we didn't have any beds and he left and took me to get some. I was so amazed that he did that because for one I was older than him. But he was a correctional officer. He sang with the group part time. I started doing hair at my apartment to pay my bills and making house calls. I tried to get a job in a salon in town with a woman who had 5 stations in her salon and was the only one in there. When she saw my work she said, "I need to sleep on it and I really don't trust these people in Belle Glade!" I looked at her and said, "Well isn't it's the people here that's paying for you to live here?" She told me to come back the next day. The next day I went, and she told me that she would rather work by herself. She was from another town in South Florida. I just continued doing hair at home. I used to go outside, and it would be this tall handsome officer standing there. Sometimes in his uniform or sometimes in his training outfit. Yes, tights from head to toe!!! I used to go in a daze and fantasize about us being together. I knew for the rest of my life I would be trying to just be in his eyesight as much as possible. I finally saw him walk and he walked liked a tall stallion horse. I wanted him, and he didn't even know I existed. It really was true love at first sight on my behalf. I knew one day I would see him again. Only he was seeing my neighbor who lived next door to me. She and her sisters lived together so I wasn't about to get triple teamed by them. But it sure felt good to look at him whenever possible. I wanted him so bad that I had dreams about him. When my godson uncle got out of jail he came and got him to live with him. My oldest daughter had her baby and it was a boy. "Wow! my first grandson," I had no son, so I was very, very happy." Later it was time for me and my daughters to part. My younger daughter became pregnant at nineteen by the singer in the group. He wasn't trying to hear that because he had a girlfriend and my daughter didn't know until she got pregnant. Later, she had my second grandson. Soon I was asked by my man to visit his family's home. His mother and father were both Christians. Sometimes I would smell like cigarette smoke and he would catch me off guard about visiting his parents. I quit smoking because I was too embarrassed when I knew they could smell it. I promised myself that I would never smoke again. He moved in with me and his ex used to send their two children over all the time. I didn't mind but I guess she thought since I was an older lady, and I had my granddaughter with me that I wanted to have more children. I became very fond of the children, why not they were his, "We thought…I'll explain later." My mom got her own place and I started going to church with his mother and family. I fell in love with his family and his mom used to cook all the time. I joined the church and started singing in the Choir. "I loved it." I promised God no more cigarettes ever again, no more cocaine, my whole outlook on life had changed for me, I was so happy. I started working in this lady salon, it was very small but at least I was in a place. She told me that she would be leaving the shop and she would leave it to me. She said she had to have back surgery and she wasn't going to be able to work anymore. Things were going great and business was great. Before she left to have the surgery, she asked me to leave the salon in her name because they wouldn't give me a license because there wasn't a back door. I didn't know any better, so I did. She said do whatever you want to the place, it's yours. So, me and my man got in there and redecorated the whole place. It was beautiful, I went to sleep that night and I dreamed that this lady told me, "Baby it comes a time when you have to change your mind." After about 2 months she came and said those exact words to me. "She wanted the place back." I was so hurt and mad. I snatched everything down and if I could have taken the paint off the wall, I would have taken that too. My man and I moved into some new apartments that the church built, and the Pastor said since we had intentions on getting married that he would rent us one. I tell you every Sunday he preached on fornication and marriage. I felt like he was talking to us. After church service so many people would ask me, "When are you all getting married?"

After living there almost a year we got married, "forcefully," only because we were living in the church apartments and they were brand new and affordable. We were married in the church hall room. My pastor came to me and said, "Have you ever thought about having your own salon?"

I said, "Yes, but I don't have the money." So, he loan me the money and I went and opened up Carletha's Beauty Salon. It had seven different rooms and me and my man got in there and hooked it up! I had a wonderful nail tech and a room where kids could play games, read, and watch TV. My man was taking before and after pictures of the customers. People from everywhere was coming for their hair to be styled and some just to see how nice the salon was fix up. They even talk about it in the city newspaper. I was so proud of myself. My youngest daughter was working with me and now she had two sons, and a crazy baby daddy!! He was selling drugs and a real thug. "A menace to society!" She left the salon one day to go get her baby from his mother's house and I told her to be careful because she was trying to get away from him. She was so afraid of him. I get a phone call saying, "I need to come to the hospital." I get there, and my daughter face was messed up. She had blood all over her blouse and big knots all in her face. I asked her what happen, and she said, "I went to get the baby and he wouldn't give him to me." She had her other son in her arm and he just started hitting her in her face. The police was already there when I got there. The same cop who arrested me when I shot at my first husband was there. When he saw that it was me being her momma, I heard him say, "Oh shit, real low." I went to go out the hospital door because I wanted his behind! The sheriff grabbed me and said, "No Carletha, let me handle this." I know how you would handle it, and you have too much to lose. I told him he better find him before I do. He had my daughter face all messed up!! I still had to maintain my business and deal with everything being crazy. My husband's ex-wife was very upset about us and decided to put child support on him. I guess she thought he had money, but he was already taking care of both children on his own. He went and told the child support people that the girl was his, but he didn't think the boy was his, even though he was named after him. He told me they said, "Well since the boy was conceived during your marriage and you don't think he's yours, let's have both children tested." The judge ordered a blood test for them both when he went to court, he told me she jumped up and said, "The boy is getting one, not my daughter!" He told me the judge said, "If you don't have them both take the blood test, I will hold you in contempt of court." So, she gave us the children for the summer, they called him to take the blood test. He went alone with the kids. About 2 weeks later he got his letter. When he walked into the salon, I knew he had been crying. I said to myself he got the results and I bet neither child is his. "It was exactly what I said." He started saying I don't want anything to do with her or them. I told him don't say that because he had been the only father that they knew. He cried and said, "I mean that, they are not mine." She called later that day because she wanted him to get her daughter clothes for school. He wouldn't answer his phone he said he didn't want to talk to her. I told him since you said it, do it, it's not the child's fault. The next time she called he told me to answer it. I answered, and she asked me where he was. I said right here, and he don't want to talk to you. She said, "He didn't say that last night." So, I said, "Well today he found out that neither child is his." She said, "What? he can't take no blood test without me!" I said, "He did, and it came back that there was 0.00 percent of blood for both." I said, "If they needed blood, he couldn't even give them any." She said, "Can you ask him to call me please." So, I guess he finally called without me knowing. So as usual, he started sneaking around, but continued telling me he wanted nothing to do with them. One day I beeped him, and he didn't call home all day. My heart started racing and I knew he was in West Palm with her and the children. When he got home, I asked him where he had been. He said his friend asked him to take him to West Palm Beach. Then he went downstairs and got in his truck. I only asked for the truth, and I would have been okay. But when you lie, you have something to hide. I went down stairs of our apartment and he was sitting in his truck. I got in and I asked him to tell me the truth. He still lied. I looked in the back and I saw brand new toys, only the boxes. They were empty. He said, "Oh, my friend brought his girlfriend's kids some toys while he was in West Palm. I said, "Okay when I see him, I will ask him." He looked at me and said I went to West Palm and went to the kid's school to see them. And I took them to the toy store. Before I knew it, I back hand slapped him. He jumped out of the truck and I had a knife in my hand, and I started chasing him around the truck trying to stab him. He ran up stairs and locked the door. I left because I had to cool off big time. Here I am trying to live as a Christian and my anger came out once again. At the time my mom and daughter lived in West Palm. I went there to my daughter's house. Later, I got upset when I found out that my man was cheating while I'm working, with this young girl, younger than him. First it was just hear say. Then one day I walked in the store and they were standing there talking and smiling, her and her mom. When he saw me, he tried to lie about their conversation, but they all were looking guilty and scared to death. I closed the salon, moved to Orlando Florida with a friend because I was afraid of what could happen. "I despise a liar." I always told him, if you don't want me anymore then it's okay with me. Just tell me. I may cry but at least you were honest. I had watched my dad cheat and had experience to much of it myself. Months later I came home to visit, and my husband talked me into coming home to him. He and his brother went to move my things back to South Bay. I was happy to come home. That same night, the same girl I suspected him of seeing came late knocking on our door. I answered the door and she smiled, "Surprise!" I went outside, I said, "I should throw your ass across this balcony." I slapped her. My husband came out and pulled me back into the house. We fussed all morning, but I wasn't going anywhere. I never mind showing the next woman that I can have my man back anytime I got ready. And plus, I had just moved back home. Soon I got the salon where I first asked the lady to work and she told me no. Things were going great. We went in and remodeled it and people were coming from everywhere, once again. My mom had got her a place back in Belle Glade and I furnish her place for her. My mom started calling me white girl. She said you think you are all that! Because I had my own business and was living good. I had my own vehicle and so did my husband. We were the talk of the town, so I name the salon TALK OF THE TOWN HAIR SALON. "Business was booming!" After the first year I decided to have the first hair and fashion show there and it was a huge success. The following year I decided to have another hair show and this time my mom was excited for me. She started hanging around me as much as she could. I used to go to the doctors with her. My husband finally got a job on the sheriff department in West Palm Beach Florida. He was on midnight shift, so he was falling asleep at the red lights driving home. So, I asked him why not just move to West Palm and I could schedule my appointments whenever I wanted to. So, we found a nice townhouse, big and beautiful. I was driving back and forth to work from West Palm to Belle Glade. The mornings were okay but driving back was terrible. I would sometimes get home at 2:00 a.m. Most of the time I didn't know how I made it home. My youngest daughter was working with me as my shampoo person. We both would sometimes be too sleepy to go home, but by the Grace of God we made it. My business was doing so good and I had mothers and daughters, and some men still wearing those jerri curls coming to get their hair done. I found out that I was doing the mother and sister's hair related to that sheriff I used to fantasize about. I knew I couldn't date him, but I sure could look at him. He started coming in to talk to his mom and sometimes when his sister was there. I would pray he would have a reason to stop by. I would stop everything and watch him from the time he walked in until the time he walk out the door. Then I would just take a deep breath and his sister would laugh at me. My mom had started sneaking me her money because she said she was tired of my brother and my niece asking to borrow her money from her little check every month and never pay her back. She told me I will come to the shop and act like I'm asking you for money, but I will slip my money in your pocket. I went and opened a savings account in my name for her. One day she was getting ready to walk out and she looked back at me and said, "I LOVE YOU." It took forty-one years for me to hear that! I ran over to my calendar and wrote down, my momma told me she love me today. I used to be mad with her and say, "You never loved me." She would say, "I love all my mother f children." "But this day was my day." I always tried to make her hug me and she would never wrap her arms around me. I would have my arms wrapped around her waist, and I would beg her to hug me back. She would ask me to leave her alone. I said Lord please don't let nothing happen to my mom because she has never told me that she loves me. Two weeks later my mom had to go into the hospital for her stomach. I asked her to pray while she was just lying there in bed. I went home that night and I fell on my knees and I begged God, please don't take my mommy. I said please lord not without her knowing you. My oldest daughter and I were visiting her, and we were sitting across from her and my mom started staring at me. She burst into tears and just kept crying. She put the sheet over her head, and she was boohoo crying. I said, "Ma what's wrong?" Then my daughter asked her if she needed a nurse. She shook her head no. So, I asked, "Ma please tell me, are you hurting?" She shook her head no. We went up to her bed and she looked at me and said, "I'm just glad," and she kept crying and I said, "What ma?" She said, "I'm just glad to know that you really did love me." I just burst out crying and so did my daughter. I hugged her and said, "Yea ma I really do." They let her go home the next day, I took her home with me and she told me she wanted to go home because I was picking up after her trying to keep my house clean. She said I was too clean for her. She started cooking and moving around good. My sister came from Georgia to see my mom, but she stayed in West Palm with me and my husband. The next day I took her to see my mom and my mom asked her to stay the night with her. My sister told her she couldn't. My mom started crying saying you can stay the night with me. She said, "Ma I got to go back to Georgia," I started crying saying, "Ma I'll stay." She said, "No you got your husband home and you already been with me." My sister left. That was the last time she saw her alive. I would go by my mom's house to check on her before I opened the salon, or if not too late, I would stop by after I closed. Her house was the house you could always go to and eat or sleep. You would sometimes see family members that you had not seen in a while, and sometimes there would be a lot of family drama. One Sunday my oldest daughter and myself and one of my brothers was at my mom house and she started talking to us. She said, "Something is fixing to happen." She said, "Ya'll better get ready!" She said, "It's not nothing bad, it is something good." She said, "God has been talking to me, and when he come for me, I'm ready to go." I looked at her and said, "Awe ma you're doing good, you're up cooking and you're looking good." She looked at me with a serious face and said, "Listen to me! I know what I'm talking about! Ya'll better get ready!" Everyday someone was always at my mom's house, but this Thursday from that Sunday, nobody stopped by to visit her. My nephew was living with her and catching the city bus to West Palm to school. This day the bus broke down on his way home. I decided to go see her that evening instead of that morning. During that day my oldest daughter called me and asked me if I could please come to her house when I finished work. I told her yes and she lived in West Palm also. That's like 45 miles from Belle Glade. My husband came by the salon in his car and I was in my car. We stopped to get gas and we headed out home. When we reached West Palm, I saw my husband turn off to a gas station, and in my mind, I said what is he doing? We already got gas, so I went on to my daughter's house to see what was going on with her. When I reached my daughter's house my husband was coming out of her house. I don't know how he beat me there. I laughed and said, "How you beat me here?" He said, "Come on Carletha, we have to go back to Belle Glade." It was about 8:00pm. I said, "No, I'm tired!" He said, "Your mom is at the hospital, she fell." I said "What!!!"

He said, "When you saw me turn off, I had a beep from your niece." He took me there within 20 min, it seemed. I was praying all the way there saying Lord please just let it be something minor. When I got there my family was there. My niece met me crying saying it was bad. They said she had 10 seizures on the way to the hospital in the ambulance. When I went in the back of the emergency room, they had my mom hooked up to everything you can name. She was foaming at the mouth and shaking. They were trying to calm her down. All I could do was break down and cry. I thought about her always telling me to never let her die at that hospital. I asked them to have her transferred to another hospital in West Palm. She remain in a coma for about 2 weeks and she would squeeze your hand when we would ask her a question when she first got there. One day we saw a tear fall from her eye. The second week the doctor told us that she was gone, and they wanted to pull the plug on her. He said if she lived, she would be a vegetable. My mom had always said if anything happened to her and she couldn't walk or do anything for herself, she didn't want to live like that. So, I was given that choice to make also. I was the youngest child, yet they act like I was the only child she had. While all of this was going on my husband was emptying my bank account. I went to the bank to deposit money in it and my mind said check the balance. It was a negative $350 dollars balance. " I was shocked." He said, "I didn't do it!" That was his answer, but there was only two names on the account, mine and his. I was making a pretty decent income. My brother had just received a lump sum of money from a settlement and he was going around wondering how much money we were putting in to help bury our mom. She had insurance since I was a little girl and we couldn't find her insurance policy anywhere in her house and that was strange. I took the money I saved for my mom and money I made and put it towards her funeral. I was mad with my husband and wanted nothing to do with him. My mother died from a company digging up ground and lying down pipes so that the people where my mom lived could start paying to use the water. A lot of houses toilets were flooding their apartments. My mom toilet over flooded and the whole apartment was full of water that reached your ankle. She was found lying on the floor coming right out of the bathroom. There were feces all over the place. She slipped and fell. I could vision her rushing trying to get something to stop her toilet from running over and slipped on some bowel movement on the floor. At my mom's funeral my husband sang, and that night before, I smoked weed which I had not done in years. I asked God to please let me be strong enough to handle this, so my husband won't come try to hold me up. At the funeral I dared him to touch me. I cried and cried but I stood on my own. When the mother of the sheriff walked up to me, she said, "I know I can't be your mother, but I will always be here for you like a mother for the rest of your life." She then said, "I love you." I felt so good hearing that from someone who had been just a loving customer of mine. I had to deal with so much. I had plan to have another hair and fashion show, but the date of the show became the date we buried my mom. During that time my oldest brother had just got diagnosed with cancer. I could not believe this. I stayed home with my husband and I had this feeling that he was cheating again. I was working all day and half the night to help make sure our bills got paid and to continue the life style we were living. He worked the midnight shift at the Sheriff Department, and I was gone all day. Things got so bad until I moved out and got my own place because we were like roommates.

Chapter 11

PREACHER MAN

During our separation my daughter ran into someone I had dated 10 years prior. He was now a minister, Wow!!! Back then he was a bartender and a drunk and snorted cocaine. She told him all the things I was going through. He told my daughter to give me his number, so he could talk to me about grieving, and help me deal with my brother suffering with the cancer. I said to myself, if he could be a minister, I know I can stay saved. I called him, and he was more than happy to come see me. I was naive, because I really thought he wanted to help me. Some of my family started going to his church and I met his wife, who loved him so much. One evening he wanted to go to the beach and talk. When we got there, he grabbed my hand and told me he had been looking for me for the last 9 years. He told me he never stopped loving me. I was shocked. I told him, "No way!! What would the people in the church think?" I joined the choir and I could see him watching me as he brought the Word. His mom and family were members there also and they knew me from when we dated in the pass. I couldn't turn for him. One Sunday I stayed home. My daughter and some friends were in church. She told me he got up in front of the church and said he wanted to make an announcement. She said he told his wife that he was sorry, but he didn't love her like a husband should and that he was in love with Carletha. He told her he wanted a divorce. My daughter said she jumped up and ran out of the church screaming and crying.

A Cry for Help

I didn't know what to do. Some of the people in the church left and some stayed. I was so embarrassed to show my face, but he convinced me everything was okay. He said it wasn't my fault. Time went on and I continued to go to church and he used to come by my house and try to sleep with me, but I refused to give in. I knew that God would not be pleased with that and I didn't love him like that. When I needed anything, he had no problem giving it to me. He started talking about when we both get a divorce then we could get married. He said I was going to be first lady and I had a special place in the church and my grandchildren couldn't sit beside me. "That was a no, no, and I didn't want it." He wanted to move in my apartment with me and continue working about 5 hours away. He didn't allow me to ask anyone to help me with nothing. He was always on time. I started thinking, Man!! I used to give away some coochie, why not? And I used to give him some years ago. But then the guilt would come in my head and say no you're better than that now. You are a Christian. He was giving me money even when I didn't ask. He was going with me to pray for my brother. This night I got on my knees and I asked God is he the one for me and I begged him to show me if I'm wrong. That night I laid down on my right side and I felt someone standing in my bedroom doorway. Somehow, I could see this big gray shadow of a man standing there. It came and laid down behind me and took a deep breath. I kept saying, "Who is you? Who is you?" Then I heard myself saying, "Jesus, Jesus, Jesus, who is you?" I tried to turn over to see who it was, but my body wouldn't move. It wrapped its arm around my waist. I screamed, "In the name of Jesus!" It got up in my ear and screamed, "WHY DO YOU KEEP CALLING ON HIM!!" I said, 'In the name of Jesus!!" Once again, I could see it leaving my room. My body just turned over on its back and I could see me up over my body looking down at my body. Then my eyes open. I was so scared. I have never seen anything close to this. I called him and told him what happen. He said it was a lust demon.

I used to come home peeping in there before I walked in. It smelled as if someone had been smoking a cigar in my apartment. I went to the office and asked them if someone had died in there. They said, "Not as they know of." I was so confused on why that would show me something about being in a relationship with him and both of us was still married and he was the Pastor. I gave in and had sex with him. It was terrible! He had no experience with making love. A waste of my time!! A month later he and I was lying in my bed and we both had on our clothes and we fell asleep. I saw my blinds roll down and I started hearing footsteps walking in my carpet. I could see myself trying to kick him and wake him up. I wasn't touching him at all. I was saying, "Pastor, Pastor he's back, wake up!" It kept walking around the bed back and forth and I was still trying to wake him up. Suddenly, it got down on its knees and I could see it watching me, but my back was turned. Then it grabbed my arm and tried to turn me around to see it. I snatched away and that's when I woke up. I hit the Pastor and woke him up, and I just cried and cried. I told him to leave so I could think. He said he had to go to work anyway. I got down on my knees and I prayed and asked God to please make me understand what to do about this situation. I said please Lord I need a speedy answer not later, right now Lord. The very next evening my niece called and said my sister that live in Georgia ex had just shot her in the stomach and they were calling the family together because they didn't think she was going to live. I called the pastor and told him what happen, and he said let me call the mother of the church and I'll rent a van, so all your family here can have a ride. I was so happy that I said, "Thank you Lord, maybe you're trying to show me that, I am to be with him." I thought I was going by myself with my family. He said, "I'm going too." My heart dropped. He was always trying to make me be submissive. He wanted to talk for me when anyone asked me a question. I told him that he didn't need to go because I didn't know how long I would be gone. Then he said, "She need some serious prayers right now." We left and went to Georgia and my sister was in ICU. She was messed up. The doctor said 1 bullet put 8 holes in her intestines. We got there, and we prayed for her and I left him in the room with my sister, so I could talk to her son. I needed to talk to my nephew because he wanted revenge. When the Pastor came out and saw me talking with him, he looked at us as if we were naked. My nephew said what's wrong with that nigga. I said nothing, he just think that he suppose to talk for me. We went and got a hotel and we were told that McDonald's was feeding the family, so we decided to go there to eat. We were going to sit in and eat, but once we got there, we were standing in line and one of the younger nephews asked me to buy him a pair of sneakers. The Pastor heard him and before I could say anything he responded and said, "Who! Who need some shoes? you better keep them you have on, I don't see nothing wrong with them." I looked at him like he was crazy because he had not seen my nephew ever in his life! I said, "I think he said Auntie!" The Pastor said, "My shoes a year old and yours look better than mine." I told my nephew I only had money for the trip. I didn't know how long I was going to be there. He said, "Okay auntie." I looked at the Pastor and he had fire in his eyes. I asked him if we were we still eating in? He said, "NO! Take me back to the room!" I grabbed my food and rushed to the van. I was on 2 wheels trying to get him there. My nephew and him got out the van once we reached the hotel and I stayed in there just thinking about what had just happen. I looked around and my nephew came and got back in the van. I asked him why did he come back? He said, "The Pastor yelled at him and said, "Gone!! Ain't she buying you a pair of shoes!!" I said, "Honey go ahead and go back to the room." He left and I drove to the other side of the hotel and cried a river. That was my answer. I made up my mind that day that God had answered me. I couldn't wait to get back home and send him on his merry way. I went back to see my sister and she told me she was tired and wanted to die. I told her to be careful what she asked God for because God can hear you. I said if that's what you really want, He will know. I didn't want her to die, so I was praying hard for her to live. Later she said she prayed to live. I had to get back home. As soon as I returned, I asked the Pastor for my door key and told him to take his toothbrush with him. He just looked at me and left my house. The next evening, he called and asked me what was going on. I told him it was over. I was going to give my husband another chance. I lied just to make him go away. He told me I was supposed to be his wife and after 10 years God had put us back together again. He said, "What God had joined together, let no man put asunder." I told him we're not married to each other. We both have different spouses. He told me he had put me before God. I told him he was a damn fool because I cannot work any miracles, only God can. Two days later my husband called me asked me if we can talk. I said sure because I figured if I'm going to go through anything, I will give my husband another chance. I still worked at my salon in Belle Glade and my brother with the cancer used to come by to see me all the time until he couldn't anymore. He used to always make my customers laugh. I had to watch his body deteriorate almost every other day. He continued to smoke his cigarettes and curse from anger, but he was fighting for his life. Father's Day was just around the corner, and my husband came by my apartment to talk and he wanted us to take a ride. We got in my Jag and he said, "I want us to go to a hotel so that we won't be disturbed." I agreed to go. He went inside to get the room while I waited in the car. He came and asked me to get out and we went on the 4th floor. When he opened the door, he had black and gold balloons all over the ceiling, champagne on ice and music playing. I was shocked!! He had already gotten the room that morning and fixed it up. We were so happy. We had a ball. After the first round we talked. I told him about the Pastor and told him I had ended it. I asked him had he been with someone and he said, "No!! All I been doing is trying to work and pay those bills." He told me he loved me, and he didn't want to spend another day without me. So, we agreed that he move in with me. Then we went for round two. I was so tired. We made some serious makeup love. After that we were knocked out. Around 10:00 p.m. someone was knocking really hard on our room door saying, "Open this door!!" Calling my husband's name. He jumped up. I then jumped up and put my pants on along with him. He opened the door. This woman walked in screaming and crying. She said, "How could you do me like this. You said you didn't want her anymore!!" I said, "Well he just told me that he loved me." He said, "And I do." She fell back on the bed and sat down. I was standing up with one knee on the bed. I said, "How long have you been seeing him?" She said, "7 months." I said, "I thought you just told me you wasn't seeing nobody?" He said, "I'm sorry." Her still crying, said, "What about my 2 boys. They love you, and I'm getting the house built." I said, "Really! Well he just told me he wanted me back." He said," I do." She jumped up and snatched a necklace from around his neck and scratched him in the chest at the same time. She sat back down and said, "I want my money back I loaned you to pay on your car." I said, "Girl you gave him money?" She said, "Yes." He said, "Well, I want my wife back if she would have me." He said, "I'm sorry if you thought we were going to be together." He then said goodbye to her. She left out screaming and crying going down the hotel hallway. I could not believe what had just happened. Talking about a man begging and pleading all night. But one thing, I'm glad she didn't want to fight because I was too tired to be trying to fight! We decided to continue with our plans. He said she went in his car at his apartment and found the receipt from the morning he got the room. The next day he started moving his things into my apartment. I put my living room suite in storage because it was white. 2 days later I was in Belle Glade working and I decided to surprise my husband and come home early. I got to the house around 4 p.m. and he wasn't home. I called his cell phone and no answer. I called it again and I heard it ringing in the bedroom as I was walking to the bathroom.

I went in the bedroom and it's lying on the bed. He never left his phone home. He was an officer. I started cleaning up from him bringing his things into my home. I found pictures of him and her and her boys. I found pictures of them at the foundation of her home being built. I even found a visiting card when he went to church with her while we were together before I left him. That let me know that all the time I thought he was cheating before I left him, that he was. I was mad all over again. I found her phone number in his phone and I called her. There was no answer. I grabbed a knife and I went riding looking for them. I didn't know where to start, but I looked everywhere. I was praying not to find them, but my mind wouldn't let me stop looking. 12:00 a.m. came and I went home. I was tired. He got home at 1:00 a.m. I had to calm down so I could hear this great lie he had to tell me. He told me that he was at a bachelor's party for one of the officers he worked with. He claim he told me. I told him that he didn't tell me nothing!!!! He kept saying he did. I told him if I find out he was with that woman, he would pay. Two months later things were going strange once again, and I couldn't believe I had taken his lying behind back. When his birthday came, I called him to tell him Happy birthday and I asked him did he get paid today? He said, "Yes." I said, "Well your gift is you getting your shit out of my house and we are surely over." I put him out of my house, and I felt good about it. He was still seeing his girlfriend behind my back and was losing the townhouse we had. He wasn't paying rent on time and her house wasn't ready yet, so he needed somewhere to go. The next week I was feeling sick. I asked my brother to take me to the emergency room. It felt like someone was sticking me in the stomach with a knife. They ran tests on me. The doctor came and said, "Ms. Carletha I need to talk to you." I told him to wait because I needed my brother in there with me. He called my brother in and he told me that I needed to wear a condom. I said, "What are you saying?" My heart was beating so fast. He said, "You have a sexually transmitted disease." He said, "Not HIV, but Trichomonas." I told him I had only been with my husband, so I didn't think I needed a condom. I told him I found out my husband was cheating on me and I left him.

He said, "You need to tell them both, they need to go to the health department." He said, "He got it from her, and he gave it to you." I called my husband the next day and I told him what the doctor said, and what he said to me was, "I didn't try to." I told him he would never ever climb on top of me again in life. I hung up and that was the end of that. It was time for another divorce. The doctors had my oldest brother put in hospice. He stayed there about a week and wanted to come home. His wife came to get him to take him home. Once she reached the house, she was trying to take him out of the car by herself, and they both fell on the ground. On Dec 31st, I went to see my brother and he was still trying to smoke his cigarette and hooked up to an oxygen tank. His breathing got worse and we called the ambulance. By the time they got there he was leaving us. I told my brother that I loved him, and he looked up at me and said, "I love you too." Right then his mouth locked, and he never said anything else. When we got to the hospital his eyes were very glossy and his mouth was still locked. Around 3:00 a.m., my oldest brother died from cancer. Within 2 yrs., I lost my mom and my oldest brother. We buried my mom 4 days before Christmas and my brother died on New Year's Day. My brother's wife told us she had everything taken care of, the arrangements for his funeral. We waited and waited. My brother was at the funeral with Incomplete wrote beside his name. I called her and asked her what was going on. She told me she didn't have any money. I was at work and some of my family members came to tell me that this homosexual guy, who was a friend of one of my younger nieces, said he was paying for my brother's funeral, and buying all the kids dresses and suits to wear to the funeral. I was told that he gave the mortician a check. They brought him by the salon and introduced him to me. I couldn't figure out why he was so generous. He asked me if I could do the obituaries.

A Cry for Help

I said, "Why are you doing this?" He said, "Because your family need help, and I just want to help y'all." I said, "Thank you." I didn't think we need help, because I always thought my brother had insurance. Later the check bounced. My daughter's godfather went and paid for everything. The same one that helped with the other family members, plus that was his wife's granddaughter that my brother was married to. The homosexual said it was a miss understanding, a wrong account. I was so hurt, two brothers gone and my mom. Later I moved in with my oldest daughter and the homosexual came by to see us. He was telling me about the Princess cruise ship and asked me if I wanted to go. I was looking for something to get into, so I started going almost every weekend on the ship with him. We became the best of friends, and I didn't understand, because he was much younger than me. He began saying that I was his big sister, and I took it at that. I began styling his hair in finger waves and we went on the ship on weekends. I was still driving the distance to work. Then one day he vanished, and I was wondering what happened to him. He called me two weeks later and told me he was locked up in the stockade. I was surprised to hear that. He began telling me about fifty million dollars he was supposed to be getting. He told me he needed a lawyer. He also said that he had all the papers documented to show the attorney. I had just moved into my own apartment, so I called an attorney and told her what he said. She asked me to go with her for the visit. He gave her the papers, and she said they were authentic. I was shocked!!!!!!!! Fifty million dollars!!! Next thing I knew, she called these two bankers in on the deal. They were so excited! They worked it out and got him on work release, saying he had a job at the bank. It worked! They gave him a nice leather brief case and a pair of shoes. He said to me, "Watch me show you how to make some crackers kiss a black man ass." The first thing I asked him was, "Are you telling the truth?" He said, "Girl yes! we are going to be rich! I am getting this money. Just stick with me. You're my sister. I'm going to buy you a big nice salon." I said, "I'm okay I just want to know if you are serious." I picked him up at the stockade and had to have him back by 5:00pm. When I picked him up for work, we would go to this big bank building on the elevator to the top floor, and they put him behind a desk with asses to a computer, "Their computer." This went on for about 2 weeks and the bankers were working on trying to get him to have the money sent to their company soon as possible. I was not working at my salon, because everyone was saying, "Don't leave him. He needs you. You are his sister." I even asked his grandmother was he for real. She said to me, "I don't know how much he is getting, but he is supposed to get a lot of money." She also asked me to please stick with him and don't allow these people to rob him, so I felt a little better. My car started running bad. The bankers would send a car to pick him up first and then me from my apartment. They would ask if we needed anything from the store or anything to eat. He would order things, but I didn't. One day he told the secretary to bring him a toothbrush. She brought it back. He just laughed. The lawyer stayed in touch and then she brought in a marketer from Miami to have a round table meeting. I didn't want to go but everyone insisted that I be there. Sitting here surrounded by all these bigtime people, who were just after that money. They were discussing how he could use the money in different areas of the market. They asked him where's the money coming from. He said that he was married to a man that was in the military and he left his Will to him that was worth fifty million dollars. They were grilling him. He was smart enough to keep them wondering. They believed him because the lawyer is the only one that saw the document and she said that they were authentic. This homosexual took me and my favorite sister to the Lexus car dealership to test drive a Lexus truck for me to use to come pick him up. He wrote a check for the total price of the truck, but they told him they had to wait seven business days before they could give him the truck, to make sure the check cleared. Thank God!!! He was getting the truck for me so I could continue to pick him up for his suppose to be job. When the attorney brought in a black marketer from Miami in on the deal, the bankers got upset. The bankers was trying to rush him into making a decision on how much money he was going to invest into their bank. They asked him to wire the money to their bank. This homosexual man went in to Kinko's, used their bank heading, and made the paper looked liked he sent the money to their bank. The banker sent the papers off to their head branch in New York, that's what he said. Later the attorney told the bankers she wanted the homosexual to only deal with the Miami marketer. Unknown to me, I found out later that, when the homosexual was in their office he went on their computer and stole money from their client's accounts. He lied and told me he was going to buy me a house and another one for each one of my two daughters. We went to Royal Palm looking at homes to be built. He had these people's mind working on really making our dreams come true. He picked out four houses. After that he went to Baer's and picked out furniture and wall paper for the house and he wrote them a check for half of the total. Soon the lawyer and the Miami man told him that they were going to take him to the bank so he could have the money wired to their bank the next morning. I was not working. So now all of my bills are due, salon and apartment. I started telling him that I needed to go to work, and he kept saying, "Don't worry I got you, I will pay them for you." The lawyer and the marketer came to pick me up first and we went to the stockade to pick him up. We went to the bank and they called him in the office. They asked me to go in with him. As I walked behind him, he turned around and said, "I got this." I went and took a seat along with the attorney and the marketer. We all watched as he was talking to the banker. Soon he came out and said to us, "Everything was taken care of." They took us back to my house and I told him I needed to pay rent at my apartment. He said, "I went yesterday and paid your rent." I said, "How did you pay it?" He said, "I wrote them a check." I was nervous about that because the one at the funeral home had bounced, also the one he wrote for the Lexus truck. I thought about the fact that I had not been to the salon going on three weeks. I told him I had to go to work. He told me to take him to the bank so he could put my name on his account, so I could pay my bills. So, my sister and I rode to the bank with him and he got out the car. I started to get out, and he said, "You don't need to go!" I said, "Yes I do because I have to sign my name." He said, "No you don't, just stay in the car and I will handle everything." "I knew he was lying about this transaction."

He stayed in the bank for about an hour, then he finally came out and gave me a card with one of the banker's name and phone number on it, a lady that knew him from Belle Glade. I called her and she told me that all he did in the bank was stand around at the table as if he was writing something. She said he took her card but never talked to anyone. After this episode, he left my house with some different guys, and he knew if he didn't make it back to the stockade by 5 p.m. he would be charged with escape. All the lies were catching up with him. The attorney called to see about him coming out for work release, and they told them that he reported back after 5 p.m., so he was not allowed to come out anymore. The attorney and the marketer came to my house the next evening and said they needed to talk to me. The marketer told me to sit down. I sat down. He told me that everything was a hoax. He said they went by the bank and talked to the lady that the homosexual had talked to and she told them that he never said anything to her about 50 million dollars. He talked to her about his brother needing an account because he had lost both of his legs and he wanted to know what he needed to do. Then he told me that he went in late on purpose. He asked the attorney, "What made you think this was real?" She said, "The papers he gave me, they are authentic." He asked her to let him see the papers and she took them out of her briefcase. He looked and said, "You went by this!" She said, "Yes." He said, "They don't even look real." "My mouth dropped." She then said, "Carletha you're the one that called me." I said, "Yea! Because you are the attorney and I am a beautician. You said they were real! Everyone went by what you said!" They left my house and all of us were looking stupid. I cried and cried because I was about to lose everything, following this person, listening to everyone saying please don't leave him, he need you, you are his sister. They made me believe because they were supposed to be the smart ones, and they believed him. He accomplished what he set out to do, and that was to make some white folks kiss a black man ass. That's what I see he did. I can honestly say I wanted to die. I prayed for God to just take the breath out of my body. I called Dr Phil show and left a message of being depressed and wanting to die. I never got a response back from his show. I asked this man to tell me the truth, so I can take my behind to work. He insisted that I would be fine. I wanted to kill his ass. You can mess with me, but not my children and my money. I never heard from the lawyer or anyone again. I was so happy because I didn't want them to think that I knew he was lying. All of us was scammed by this person. My friend who worked on the cruise ship told me to come go to the Bahamas with him to get away because I was so depressed and couldn't stop crying or worrying about my bills. I went and I asked God to let the ship sink and I drown. We left 1:00 am. The next day I went on deck and I saw nothing but the ocean. I was so scared because that is one of my worst fears, drowning. "All that water!" I ran inside and started asking God, "Please, don't sink the ship." I went home and called my youngest daughter who was working with me. "Wanting to die, unknown to me God had went before me and made my crooked path straight." I told my daughter to see if the lights were still on and the water. She said, "Yes." I told her to check the messages and I had 35 messages where people wanted to get their hair styled. She cleaned the salon. We called those people and I took my butt to work. God made it possible for me to pay all of my bills at my apartment and the salon. "I was so happy He didn't allow me to die in the ocean." I could not believe that when it came time for the homosexual to get out of jail, he called me and asked me if he could come and spend the night with me. I could not believe that he had the nerve to come around me. I thought, "now I can kill him." I told him, "Yes." I never heard from him within the time he scammed everyone, until this phone call, almost a year later. He came that night he called, and he fell asleep on my couch. When he opened his eyes, I was standing over him with a knife. He jumped up and started talking fast. I really only wanted to scare him to death, because I had too much to lose. I told him he better get out of my house and never come around me or my family ever again!!! I said, "If you see me anywhere!!! You better turn and look the other way!" I decided to look around in West Palm for a salon to work in because it was hurting so bad being there since my mom and brother had died. I found a salon that was just opening in a real busy plaza, and she had eight stations with only two girls working in there. She was just as happy as I was to be there. I started working in there and learning new techniques from the younger girls and new styles. Soon we had eight stations filled, and two nail techs. I was the oldest of everyone except the owner. She only sat all day and made appointments and watched her money. I was not accustomed to working on commission. "The lady who we were working for was making a killing from our hard, earned money." We had a beauty supply store two doors down from us that was owned by two brothers. They loved me because I was making them a lot of money. I used to weave my own hair then walk in their store so people could ask me who did my hair. Soon the brothers started sending customers to me. I started asking the owner of the salon, why not let us rent our station so we could pay our bills at home. She refused to for a long time until I threatened to leave. The other girls said, if I left, they were leaving too. So finally, she agreed, and then asked me if I would be the manager. I came up with so many of my own hairstyles and they were selling. This man came and wanted to Debut the hairstylists of West Palm and I was the only one in our salon that participated. I had five models. Of course, two of them were my daughters. There was a huge crowd that showed up at the Marriott hotel. I invited my family, but my dad was the only one that showed up. The people loved all my hairstyles but this one style I created on one of the ladies that worked with me, made the whole audience stand up. Yes, I got a Standing Ovation!! When she walked away, they began shouting," Come back!!!! Come back!!! Come back!" She went back and the people were clapping like crazy. They wanted the stylist to come up on the stage with her. "THAT WAS ME!" My dad had tears in his eyes. He gave me a big hug and said, "You know you can do some hair!" He said, "I am so proud of you." That was a dream come true for me. At this present time in my life, I was living the single life. One of my home brothers was working with a linen company that delivered towels and rugs for the salon. I began renting from them to help his business grow. He had a friend that was from his home town that was an ex NFL player. The last time I saw him he was about 12 or13 years old. Yes, that same little boy that used to stare at me, that lived next door to my baby's grandmother. He came to visit. My brother brought him by the salon, and we were shocked to know each other from the past. He lived in Tampa, Florida. He would come to town to visit me and I would go to Tampa to see him. My friend/brother didn't agree with us seeing each other because he didn't want me to get my feelings hurt, because they were good friends from child hood, and friends know what friends do. I continued to see him when time permitted for the both of us. As I continued to find something at home, because each town furnished their own men and women, we would always call each other to just see how the other one is doing; after we both got busy in our careers. He had to work, and so did I. I was not moving to Tampa and he was not moving to West Palm. One night my nephew came in with this gorgeous hunk of a man and all the girls got extra frisky. He had those big hazel eyes. Only he had been in there once before with a wife and two kids. I was the one who did his wife's hair. My nephew introduced us and when he smiled, I just melted. He asked if he could take me out to dinner and I asked, "Where is your family?" He told me she left him and told him to find someone else because she was moving to another county, and she was gone. I thought I had just won the lotto. I told him yes. Of course, there was envy in the salon that he chose the oldest person in there, a grown and sexy woman. We started dating. We went everywhere together. I used to take him on the ship with me and women would forget they were already with someone. They would stare, and I would feel jealous, but never showed it. He soon showed me where he had an operation on his brain.

They had to take part of his brain out. In my mind I was scared because I didn't know what mind framed he was in with part of his brain out. I said, "Oh shit!" In my mind of course. He always wore his caps to match his outfit, so I never notice it. Hell, it was dark in the bedroom. He said he was injured in the military. Sometimes he would get these real bad headaches and he would just lye back in my lap for hours and just sleep while I rubbed his head. I didn't mind because I was falling head over heels for him. He was so sweet, and his voice would just woo you. He took me to meet his mom and dad, and they were the nicest people I could have ever met. I told them I had 2 adult daughters and 8 grandchildren. This man was just starting with his own small children. My grandchildren were older than his children. One day he came over with his son. We had a ball. The son told his mom about his honey, that's what his little boy would call me. Then one day I looked, he had both kids. He said she told him he could keep both of his children, while she pursue her career. I didn't see him that often, but we were making it work. She started questioning him about me. And he told her the truth. He said she threaten to take the children and not let him see them anymore if he didn't stop seeing me. He told me he was torn because she left him and told him to find someone else. I guess she didn't think it would happen so fast, and he was also a sharp dresser like me, (ha,ha,). "I was in love, that's all I can say." "Wow if only you can see the future." One day his mom called me and told me he was shot, and to come to the hospital. I rushed to the hospital and his family was there, and his wife. She noticed then, that I was the same lady who had style her hair prior. He was shot in the shoulder and told the police that he shot himself. Then his mom asked me if I knew he was doing drugs. I said, "Doing drugs!!! Not ever around me." I know he was on medication, but not street drugs. They found cocaine in his system. He stuck to saying he shot himself. They sent him to the VA hospital for therapy and treatment. I couldn't see him because he was still married. When he got out about a month or two later, he came to my daughter's house in a nice BMW and told me it belong to one of the nurses that was taking care of him at the VA hospital. He told me that she was always there talking to him and wanted to date him. He told me she was going to be the way he come up. If I had a bomb, I would have blown him and her car up. That's how I felt at that time. He asked me to just hold on and be patience because she had plenty of money, and she didn't mind spending it on him. I told him to get out of my face and don't ever bring that bitch car back around here again. I tried to work but I couldn't think straight. I waited on this man to get well for him to tell me this. He came again a week later, in her car again, trying to tell me how he loved me and missed me so much but wanted to still, as he says, use the other chick. I couldn't take it anymore more. My heart was shattered. I called my nephew and his wife in St. Petersburg, FL and asked if I could come live with them until I find my own place there. They said yes. I left the town, the salon, the grandchildren and all, before I hurt someone. I didn't want to go back to that person from my past. I got a U-Haul and moved on. While I was there, I called my friend in Tampa to let him know that I was very closed to him. He came in his nice truck and picked me up. I stayed the weekend with him, not just to have sex, because we knew one another, and he use to talk to me about things going on with him and I did the same. Most of the time he would just sit and hold me. I saw his beautiful home and all he had, but that was just stuff to me. He told me he noticed me when I was living next door to his mom in Pahokee, FL. He was 12 and he use to say to himself, boy when I grow up, I'm going to get her and keep her for myself. I just laughed because then I had to be 18 or 19 years old, "but I was always small and sexy." I told him I saw him but as a little boy with a snotty nose. We would laugh. "Things were not going as I planned, and things started looking crazy for me in St Pete." I would come home to visit and when I got ready to leave, my grandchildren would run behind the car calling me saying, "Don't leave." I would cry sometimes all the way back to St. Pete. Can you imagine how many customers I let down and left them depending on someone else to take care of their hair? "Trust me it wasn't the same." After a few months there, I decided to come back home. I went back to the salon to work and things were going good once again. The owner told me that if she decided to sell the salon, she would ask me first since I was the manager. Then here he comes, (trouble). More now on cocaine then before I left. I wanted no part of him or that drug ever again. I promised God a long time ago, no more in this lifetime, not even a cigarette, but I was still smoking weed. That was like medicine to me. Something I thought I needed to sleep and not dream about anything. I started going out to my friend/ brother's night club at the Hilton. I became the decorator for the club for him when he had different events and holidays. I loved doing that. People used to walk in the club and be amazed. I began styling his daughter's and his wife's hair. And after his club we would go to the hood club, because it stayed open the longest. I called it the hole in the wall club. You could eat chicken wings and dance your heart out. I love to dance. I could still dance my behind off. All the single men eyes were all on me and I loved the attention. One night I met this handsome, dark skinned man who looked just like Morris Chestnut. He was built just like him. He was younger than my daughters. I was older than his momma. Eye contact and it was on. Well, the owner decided to sell the salon only she sold it to someone else. She came to me and said she was still part owner and she wanted me to stay and work with her partner. I thought about it until the new owner and her mom came in and her mom said, "This is my daughter's salon and she is the only owner and whoever do not want to stay give us your key and leave!" I had already scoped out an empty salon, but it was far away from there. The dealer who sold me my car knew the guy who owned the salon. It was in a big beautiful plaza. I packed my things. Two stylist and the two nail techs left with me. We opened the salon and I called every client that I had a number for, to let them know that I had moved. The mother of the sheriff and the sister and the sister's daughter started coming back to me because now I was now closer to them from Belle Glade. All those years I hadn't seen them or him. God brought back my mom and friend. A lot of my customers I had in Belle Glade started coming back to me. I was so happy to see them because that was home. Yes!! Mr. (the sheriff) started coming in there to see his momma once again and was still fine as ever. Now I get to see him in casual clothes, and he wore them well!! His mom would just laugh at me because now I am single and I let him know that he was breath taking, at least he was taking mine. He would look at me and blush. Wow what a smile!!! I was still smoking my weed, "I couldn't date a cop!" I put Mr. Chestnut look alike on hold until I took care of my business. "Still wanting and looking for love in all the wrong places." Just wanted the love I didn't get as a child from my father. I guess you'd say, I never give up. Well, Morris Chestnut look alike had two small children and a wife that wanted a divorce. She moved out of state with the children, so, I figured no baby momma drama, not at this age in my life. I really wanted to have him when I got ready, not a relationship. I got tricked into this relationship. He asked me if he could move in with me until they finish his house that he and a cousin were supposed to move in. He said it would only take about two weeks because their lease was up. Two weeks never came. We ended up moving into a town house together and was doing okay. This man had a huge family of just men. He had 5 brothers, one who was at the time playing with Tampa Bay Buccaneers. All of them were sweethearts, but you could see a little jealousy here and there. My new friend's ex wanted us to keep the children one summer, and I'm okay with that because kids are not responsible for their parent's action. He told me that she was always telling him to tell his sugar mama hello, or you with that old ass woman. But we were happy most of the time until he goes out with his cousin and come home drunk. Dead drunk, can't walk, can't talk, vomiting all over the house. Then when I tell him I never want a drunk he wants to apologize, until the next time. I was once again a real house wife without the ring. I was working at my salon which I named "Off the Chain Hair and Nail Studio." I was trying to take care of everything and everyone. I started gaining weight and hated going home because if he wasn't getting drunk, he was playing football on the play station all day when he got off from work. He had a good job, and yes, I got that check!! His ex called one day telling me that he promised to send her money to help with her son, not his son. She was upset because he hadn't sent it. I told her, honey he don't have any money, once he give me money to help pay these bills, he is almost broke. And I said and he surely don't have a sugar mama. She told me he said I didn't want her calling to the house. I said, "Yes, I said it. If anything, the kids can call you when they are here and he can talk to you on his job when the kids are not here." She said, "Well I didn't want him and when I did have him all we did was fight. I asked God to get me out of that mess and He did." She said, "There is not one bone on his body that I want." I said, "Well good!!" I got where I hated to come home to him. Soon his brother who played in the NFL came to live with us, him and his girlfriend. I felt so much better and things went good for a while. He had a more laid back attitude. He wasn't with all that silliness. I came up with a plan. I told him that I would go to St. Petersburg, FL for a month or two and work there then come back home. He really didn't understand that but living there was too intense and leaving him completely was too intense. I started staying with my daughter more and talking with her and looking at my grandchildren. I thought it was time to leave him completely. My daughter was out of town with the church one Sunday. I took my second oldest granddaughter with me. I told her if anything happens, to go outside on the patio. I went to get my things out of the town house. When I got there, he was mad because I wanted my things, so he started cursing and helping me get my things together. I got even madder because he was helping me. Then he made a statement like you almost dead anyway, meaning my age. Then I said with your little dick ass. Then I looked back and my granddaughter was standing on the stairs. I screamed and told her to go outside on the patio!! While I was packing his ex-wife called and I answered the phone. She told me that he told her that I was moving out of town and he wanted them to get back together. She claimed that she told him it would never happen. He came and snatched the phone out of my hand and told her she don't have to talk to me that he would call her later. I don't know why he brought the beast out of me! I grabbed the long neck bottle off the table and hit him on his arm because he blocked his face. I saw blood on his arm, and I knew I had busted it open. I screamed and told him you don't know who you're messing with!!! I called the police and told them I was trying to get my things and he was trying to stop me. I thought I had hung up the phone when I told him that I will kill him. He told me he was going to tell his momma. I told him I would beat his momma ass!! Then I punched him in the mouth and his lip started bleeding. He picked up the phone and he said hello, and the police was still on the phone. He called me later and told me that the police heard me say that I would kill him. He told me that you better be glad I don't want to have you locked up. I told him to do what you're going to do!! After 2 years that was over! During this time my best friend/brother was in the process of opening up his own club partnering with a two time world boxing champion and his father. I helped him with getting it ready and all the decorations. It was beautiful. I decorated the whole club and it was huge. My friend/brother let me work the door for him. I was happy to take the money at the door because that area was outside the whole club. I was so happy now, working my salon, participating in different hair shows, and winning a lot of them. I was so excited when I finally made it to a Bronner Bros hair show in Atlanta Ga. I did the same hairstyle on the same lady who worked with me that I got a standing ovation on and I tell you so many people there was following us taking pictures and asking all kinds of questions. I felt like I was a part of the show. Some of the star stylists were asking me about my hairstyle. They told me that I needed to be on stage beside them and traveling designing hair. Another hair show I participated in was in Orlando, FL. It was a competition. I did evening wear. They wanted the model to be dressed from head to toe. There were two judges during the break came to find me and asked me how in the world did I come up with that hairstyle? One was from Canada, a man and the other was from Italy, a woman. They told me next time to do real clothing because the other judges said the dress looked like a costume. I had her dress made of garbage bags. It was beautiful. The lady judge from Italy told me she wished I could come back to Italy with her and do this hairstyle. They told me that they voted for me but didn't know how it was going to go. One thing that I learned in competing in hair shows in someone else home town, is that it's not what you know, it's who you know. Out of 17 girls they gave me 7th place. I was disappointing with all the monies I had spent for hotel and to enter the contest. But at least I got to be seen and talked about, good or bad. One lady saw the garbage bag dress and told me to please get in touch with the company and let them see what I had done. I entered into another hair show in Miami, and that was the last straw! Everyone there knew each other by name. But my mind is always working on something new when one thing fail. I even came up with an invention for bonding hair. I went through one of the invention companies and I paid money down for them to research and do my book that tells you about me and my invention. Then they had me paying so much money monthly. They gave me my invention book which named me as an inventor. Real nice, but I felt like I was buying my own invention. I went to their office and the guy asked me, "What did you come here in, your limo?" He's telling me to send my package to Oprah and Beverly Johnson, and Jet Magazine. There was also a list of those who thought it was a great idea. They forgot that I had to work and pay them all that money to do nothing. I asked him, "What am I paying them for every month. He had me so hyped up. He was telling me to go find my dream house and I was going to make plenty of money from my invention. A year went by and they wanted me to make another down payment, another thousand dollars. They wanted me to start making payments all over again. That was not happening. I still have my idea in my head and whatever is meant to be will be. Back to the club, its grand opening night and here come the New Yorker's. The club was a huge success. The father of the boxer was around my age and the family got to know me from asking questions about who had that much talent to decorate and design the VIP room. I was holding down the door with a line of approximately 3 miles long. Everyone who was everyone was hanging out there. There was star entertainment in there. Betty Wright, Petey Pablo, Ying yang Twins etc.... I got my body in shape and had a dressed code that wouldn't wait. Sometimes there were strip shows. Everyone was running at the dad and the dad was smiling at me. I was running from him because at last I'm single and free. Didn't want a relationship and wasn't looking for one. Then one day one of his sons and my youngest daughter thought that we should formally be introduced. They didn't know that we had briefly talked before. We just went alone with it and one thing lead to another. When I tell you, those women were after him!! I just remained who I was and did my job. Soon my big brother/friend got the news that I was talking to the father and he came to talk to me about him. He told me that employee and employer could not see each other. I told him this man is grown and so am I. The father and I both made an agreement that we wasn't looking for love just a friendship and just see what happens. Then he told me that the father only slept with trash. So, I talked to the father about what he said, and he was shocked. Then he told me that my friend/brother told him that he wanted me gone from the club and I was lazy and couldn't keep a man. He told him that it had to be me that was the problem that I was single. Then I was shocked. 15 yrs of friendship and like a brother to me. His wife was calling me ma. I was now babysitting their daughter and doing their hair. Everything was about to crumble between us. I continued to work there, and my brother and I was friendly to each other. He knew he could trust me with his money, and he was making a lot of money!!! One night my ex from Tampa showed up as a VIP guest. He asked me if I could talk to him after the club. I told him no. Only because I was seeing the father and he was in town. He said please!! I really need to talk to you. I told him I was sorry, but I couldn't. He had moved to another state and he was telling me he would send me a ticket there to visit him. I said, "I can't. I'm seeing someone." He just looked at me and smile. Months later I heard on the news that he had shot himself in the head, in his Tampa home. He had developed an injury on his brain from playing professional football, so I heard. I sometimes wonder today if that's what he needed to talk to me about. I was shocked and so sad, still today. The father told me to stop working there and everything would be just fine. That made me very sad, that all the years of thinking someone really cared, then turn around and make you feel like they only cared about what you did for them. Soon the father's family moved here, and we became closer. They started training down south. I used to get off from work and head down south to be with him. They had a habit of staying up all night and sleeping half of a day, then train. I used to be so tired and sleepy because sometimes I had to work and had been up all night, but I would handle my business. I always said I would never fly because of my fear of height. But when you think you are in love with someone you would try to swim in the middle of the ocean to see them. We were in this relationship now almost a year and he sent me a plane ticket to come to New York. At first, I was scared but I hadn't seen him in about a month. Honey! My daughter took me to that airport, and I acted like

I had been flying all my life. I was so excited to see him. I didn't even care that it was at night. He treated me like a queen. Every time we went to the gym everyone would ask if I was his wife, and he would look at me and smile and say yea. I couldn't believe at last I'm dating someone my age. Only he act like he was 25 and his family thought that I thought I was young. We had fun and enjoyed each other. He even took me up in the CatSkill Mountains. I saw a sign that said Utica, New York, 50 miles. I was so excited because that's where I had not been many, many years. I was there for 2 weeks and made it back home safe. Time to get to work. My oldest daughter went to Cosmetology school and got her license. She went from nursing to hair styling. She surprised me. That woman could do some hair!!! She was holding things down every time I was missing from the salon. She sometimes had to do her customers and mine. He was talking about getting me an apartment when he come back down, but when he came back, I was already in my apartment with my own money. He was surprised when he called me, and I gave him my new address. I had a one bedroom that was just the right size for me. My youngest daughter found me a dog to stay with me. I wore a lot of blond wigs because the father said he liked them, so my daughter found me a blonde haired dog. My dog did not like him or anybody besides my oldest daughter. Not even the daughter who found him. That was my protection while I had to be there alone. Mr. NY loved taking me places and doing things for me, but also loved the fact that I was an independent woman. He was into a different religion than me. We discussed it before, but never debated about it. He was getting ready to leave FL because his son had a big fight that weekend and this night we was riding from Miami and I said, I really thank you Jesus for loving me. And he said to me, "Jesus ain't shit." I said to myself, "Oh my God, please don't flip this truck over!" He was driving and I said, "You better take that back!!" He then said, "Jesus ain't what everybody scrap him up to be. Jesus was just a prophet. He did not get all beat up and he did not die and come back." I then told him you believe what you want, and I will always believe in Jesus. I told him I was born and bread, Jesus Christ, and we agreed to disagree. He dropped me off to my apartment and I said have a safe flight. That same weekend his son had a big fight against an unknown fighter in his home town. Guess what, he lost!! His home town was upset with him for losing that fight. I was so hurt for him and his son, but I knew why it happen. This is my opinion. God said, "You talked bad about my son, and only one person heard you, but let me show you what I can do to your son in front of the world and his home town. While he was gone, I was a mentor for his niece who is 13, who said when she grew up she wanted to be a hairstylist. Her mom was so happy for her. I would allow her to come in after school and on weekends. She became my shampoo person and she became so good at it that the customers were requesting her. My sheriff was still walking in and out even while she was there, and I just couldn't refrain myself from saying something to him. He would still just blush. Just because you're with someone else don't mean that you went blind. I knew how far too go. I used to spend a lot of time with his family from NY that had moved here. Another year went by and we were still hanging in there. He was still living in New York and I was still here. I would go visit him and sometimes he would be here a month or two, or however long it took to train his son. Now his nieces decided to call me auntie, all of them that lived here. I was surprised, but that's what they wanted to call me. I loved them so much. I became very close to the niece that worked with me. One day I dropped her home and she said that her grandmother asked if I was with her. She said she said no, and the grandmother said, "Good!!" I was shocked because she always would tell me to come by and sit with her sometimes. Then it was time for her to go to school. My daughter and I went and brought her some clothes to show our appreciation and she said her grandmother got upset because we did it. She really didn't want us to think that they couldn't buy her anything. The niece told me that when I would leave the house, that they would talk about me. For one, saying, "She thinks she is young!!!" But that was so far from our minds. We always liked helping people. One day my brother came to my house and told me that our dad was in the hospital. To be honest, I really didn't care. I said, "Ok, I don't care." I hadn't spoke to my dad in a year from him talking very negative about my baby brother to his daughter. A few days later my brother came back and told me that the doctors didn't think that he was going to make it because his system was poisoning his whole body. He told me that he asked about me. So, I decided to go see him. When I walked in, he stared and started crying and said, "I was wondering if you were coming." I looked at him and he was very sick and weak. I started crying with him and said, "You know I was coming." I had never seen him like that. I don't even remember him ever being sick. While I was there, I noticed that my brother was driving my dad's car and living in his house. My younger brother that my daddy raised was there also. We talked about what's going to happen if he died, and he said daddy said that he didn't want to be cremated. So, I asked him if he knew whether or not daddy had any insurance. He said he didn't know. I told him to ask our dad. He said, "No, I can't ask him that!" I said, "Why not? You say you love him." I told him if he didn't have any that he would be cremated. I told him, "I don't have any money. He took my money when I was younger, and you don't have any money to bury him." I said, "You need to ask him about his insurance!" He said, "You ask him. You are bolder than I am. I said, "Ok." Later we went back to my dad's room and I asked him if he had insurance? He looked at me and said, "I'm glad you asked." Then he said, "NO." I turned to the hospital window and I cried like a baby. Here it is, my brother and I were the two oldest out of 18 or more children that my dad claimed he had, I don't know but 7. We are to make all the decisions. My brother is telling me that my daddy said he never want to be cremated. A few years back he told me that he was thinking of having a live funeral. So, my question is, how was he going to pay for that? I left and my brother remained there still driving my dad's car. I was sitting home after a long day at work and my brother knocked on the door. When I looked through the peep hole, I already knew what he was about to tell me. I opened the door and he walked in and he looked at me and said he is gone. For a minute I was so confused about my feelings for him, after all he was my daddy. When my brother left, I cried all night. Reminiscing about him wasn't anything good I could think of, certainly not with me and my baby brother. I even thought about one of his exes telling me before she died, that she knows that my dad poisoned her before. She said after he poisoned her, he tried to have her committed into a mental health center, telling them that she tried to kill herself. I don't know if she was talking about in the past when they were together, or later, she didn't say. She was very sick at the time she told me. I went to visit her, at her house. After she told me that, it wasn't long before she died. My heart was so heavy. I wish she had never told me. But, I knew he was capable of doing that to someone. I believe there were others, but I can't prove it. When the doctor said that his system was poisoning his whole body, I thought about the saying, (You live by the sword, you die by the sword.) When he died it was on a week day, and I had to work. My scheduled was filled up till that Saturday. That Friday my brother came to my salon and sat down and told me that my dad's daughter and he had talked about the arrangements for our dad's funeral. He told me that she said she already had a casket, a church, the suit, and the funeral owed her a family flower. I was like dang!!! That's alright. He said he talked to the funeral home director and he said he would help us because he and my dad were good friends. He said she asked him to come by and see if I had any money to help. I told him, "I don't have any money. All I have is my bill money." I said, "Tell her I can do the obituaries if she wanted me too." He said, "Well she wanted to meet with us Monday at daddy house so we could discuss the arrangements." I said, "No problem. I'll be there." I was like, he sure did show her some love!!! I had not seen this sister in many years, and my daughter and I left West Palm Beach, FL and went to Ft. Pierce, FL to meet them at my dad's house. We were the first one to get there and the door was opened. My daughter and I went in and the house was so junky, almost like the show, Hoarder. Soon my sister and her husband, at the time, walked in and we all hugged each other with a smile. I was happy to see her all grown up. Then we took a seat looking at each other and having small conversations, waiting on my brother to show up.

We waited and waited and waited. He never came. So, before it got too late, I broke the ice and said, "Ok, this is what our brother said." I told her everything he had told me she said she was going to do.

She screamed, "WHO!!!" She said, "I never told him that! He wasn't no father to me!!" I said, "WHAT!!" My daughter was my witness and a few customers when my brother told me all of that. I told her how I used to be envious of her and my dad's relationship because he said he was with her every Thanksgiving. She said, "I didn't invite him, he just showed up at my house." She said when she was little she was in the hospital and he was outside her room and a nurse asked him was he her father and he said, "No I am her grandfather." She said, "He didn't want to be billed for her hospital bill." We started looking for anything in the house that could help us bury him. He told me a while back that he worked at the Sheriff Department. I called to see if he had any insurance with them. They said, "No ma'am, he was a citizen on patrol." Then I found an ID he had for the Military. I called them. He's never been in the military. We kept searching, and then we came across 3 different ID's with 3 different names. Only the last name was the same. I just screamed and said, "WHO IS THIS MAN!!!!" I just found out on accessory.com that he was born in Cuba! I don't know where they get their information from. He was an only child and his 2 aunts I knew were dead. When I did finally talk to my brother, later that week, I told him what our sister said, and he told me she was lying. Then he got upset and said, "Don't worry about it. I'll take care of everything myself!!" I said, "You're going to take care of everything?" He said, "Yea!!" I said, "Okay." Then we hung up. The next week I got a phone call from the son my father raised, and he was furious. He said my brother had took the car and had the police to remove him from the house. I couldn't believe my ears. He started crying. I told him I would call our brother and talk to him. When I called him, I told him what was said and he told me, in other words, to mind my own business; then hung up on me. He was hot with me!! I think the car held up for about a month, then it broke down on him. The next week I was driving by and he was at a bus stop and I blew my horn at him. He turned his back to me and I cried half the night. We had never been at odds with each other, not like this. Well time went by and a month and a half later I got a call from my sister with the mortician on their way. He told me that my dad's body was still there, and he was getting ready to send the sheriff at my brother for an abandon body. I was shocked!! I said, "Sir, my brother told me that he was going to handle everything, so I stepped back. He said, "I've never seen your brother. He said, "Your brother called me a day before your dad died and asked me when he die, could I pick his body up. And I told him yes, but I never met him." I said, "Sir, tell me what you need from me." He already knew my sister, so he said my dad had money in his bank account and that would be enough to cremate him. I then asked my sister if she can go get the money. The mortician said that he could get the money with no problem. He just needed someone to sign the papers. So, I ask my sister to please go for us and do at least that much for daddy. I don't know where his ashes is or anything, and it haunts me at times. The next year, on Father's Day, I cried and cried, looking up to heaven praying that he asked God for forgiveness because he sure didn't ask me. I screamed, "GOD WOULDN'T ALLOW ME TO HAVE MONEY TO BURY YOU!!! I'M SORRY!!!! I'M SORRY DADDY!!" I felt so sad that I wanted to help the world if I could. One day this lady called from a homeless shelter and asked me if I could style the homeless mothers' hair for job interviews. I told her of course I could do that. She said they don't have any money. I said I know and that's fine. The lady was shocked. She said she had called a lot of salons and each one of them told her no. She was so happy. She kept saying thank you so much. I even mentored other seniors in high school and let them know to never give up no matter what happens in their life. Time went on and the father, Mr. NY, had a big fight in Vegas. He asked me if I wanted to go with him. Of course, I said yes. He said I could hang out with his mom and sisters. That was said a month before the fight. Time was coming up to go. Suddenly, the family isn't going, but they decided that I could still go by myself. He kept saying I will be at the gym most of the time training. So, I said, "Well, I can stay home." He said, "No, if you really want to go then I'll get you a ticket." He said, "You will have to fly by yourself because I have to leave a week before you." I was so scared. I had only flown to New York. This was 5 hours in the air at night. I couldn't understand why they were staying. I went on the plane, and on the flight, I met one of Don King's men. That's what he told me. I told him who I was going to see, and he showed me how to take the train to baggage and he waited with me because once I got there, I was alone. No one was there to meet me. Then the man said oh that's where I'm going. I could give you a ride to his hotel. I said no because I really didn't know him. I've seen him on tv, but that's it. I waited almost thirty minutes. I had to call my oldest daughter in Florida, so she could contact him to let him know that I had made it. He called my phone and told me to catch a cab at this hotel, and he had made reservations for me. The cab dropped me off and I go into this hotel, stand in line, and get to the desk, no reservations! Now I'm pissed and scared. I'm 3000 miles away from home all alone. I called him and he told me to hold on he was coming. 30mins later he walks in. Got me a room, gave me money, walk me to my room, and told me to come back down stairs to play the slot machines. I had never liked gambling, but I went down later after my shower. They were still there playing a few slots. He called me over to a machine to play a game with him. After about an hour he kissed me and told me he had to go back to the gym. He told me that I would not see him that much because he had to train his son. He told me to come to the hotel the next day for the interview with the fighters. I caught a cab to the hotel where they stayed, and I got on the escalator to go down where he was, and he was talking to a white lady who could have been a reporter. The interview with the fighters was over. Somebody gave me the wrong time. When he saw me, he turned his head and he and the lady got on the escalator to go up the stairs. I called his name and he ignored me. I got on the escalator and went up too. I was walking behind them, and they turned to go into a restaurant. As they were standing in line, I asked him, "Do you need for me to go back to my room or what!!!" I was getting ready to show him a side of me that he had never seen. Then he looked at me and said, "Yea." I called a cab and I went back to my room and I cried and cried and cried. All I could think about was how could you have me to leave home from my family and you brought the ticket. I called him and told him I wanted to go home. He said, "I thought you wanted to see the fight?" I said, "you pretend you didn't even know me," he said no, "I was talking to the reporter." I said, "I don't care who that was I'm too far away from home." He told me that my ticket for the fight would be waiting at the ticket booth and money for me to pay extra to come back home. I knew from him treating me bad from the start that at least I would be closed to the ring. When I got my ticket, I was in the nose bleed section. I was shocked! I didn't have to be on the floor but at least an area I could see good. Some of the men that were up there started a conversation with me about the fight and was shocked when I told them I was the girlfriend of the father. They asked what the hell you doing up here? I was so embarrassed. I called my daughter that night when I reached my room and I cried. She said, "momma all I want you to do is make it home and I will be at the airport waiting on you with open arms." I cried all night and I prayed for God to please get my stupid behind home. I got on that plane and didn't look back. I never took my seat belt off and I slept all the way home. When I reached Ft Lauderdale Airport, I was coming down that escalator looking for my daughter and her husband feet!!! I wanted to do like Richard Pryor in that movie. KISS THE GROUND!!!!!! I said never again!!! Not with him! I found out later it was because he had another woman with him the whole time. I wouldn't answer his phone calls and I didn't call him. I just concentrated on my business and church. The next month he popped up at my salon, him and his brother. He asked me to please come outside so he could talk to me. I went out there and I told him how I felt. And I asked him, "how could you have me come so far from home from my daughters and grandchildren and treat me like that." He tried to act like he didn't remember him acting like he didn't see me. He just kept saying he was sorry and asked if he could come by my apartment later to talk to me. I wasn't feeling him that was not that easy to forget. So, no I didn't, I had to be hard and let him feel me. I continued to help his niece as much as possible and visit his family only when I was invited. A few months later he called me and told me he missed me and wanted me and his mom to come to New York together. I was not sure about going until he said me and his mom. He told me that he had a surprise for me. So off we went. When we arrive to New York we went to his house and he took me to get a pedicure and my nails done. It was cold! He told me he loved how I decorate and asked if I could decorate his bathrooms for him and some other parts of his house. "That was just conversation." He took me out bowling where all the stars go bowling and we ran into Fabulous and I took a picture with him. Then he took me out to have a nice dinner. My daughter called to see if I was okay and he asked to speak to her, he told her I got your mom and she will be happy when she come back home. My daughter said, "thank you." I told her that I was okay. I stayed for 4 days and it was just too cold for me and it was raining with it. He told me he had to go to work the next day so I left his house in a cab to go to the airport, I thought he was on a race track, I can't count how many accidents he almost had, I was glad to get to that airport. I was standing in line to get my ticket and I heard over the intercom, flight to West Palm Bch Fl has loaded and ready for takeoff. I was like no!! That's my flight!! I dropped my bag and just stood there in a daze. When I got to the window, they told me that I missed my flight. I said, "mam the line was so long." She said I could catch a straight through tomorrow morning. I went looking for a phone with this big roller bag. I felt like Ciecly in the color purple, I could have just stood there and fainted. They said I had to go down stairs to the bottom floor for a phone booth. My cell phone would not work. I didn't have any change, I was dragging that bag all over the airport, up and down on the elevators. "I wanted to cry like a baby." When I was in the elevator for the third time it was two guys that worked at the airport saw me looking lost and stressed out. They asked me, "are you okay?" "I wanted to burst out crying saying no!! I don't know where I am, and I wish someone would just steal my luggage and I need change!!! But I was calmed, I said, "no I'm fine, thank you for asking." I finally found a shop to get change. I kept calling his cell phone and it wasn't going through. I was hoping that someone would steal my big bag because I was tired of pulling it. I had to call my daughter for her to call him, he called me back and came to pick me up. The next morning, I was on a Delta plane with 15 people only. I knew it was the end of us seeing each other on a regular because I was still upset with him, but still cared a great deal for him. I prayed all the way home because I had never been on a plane that early, or that empty. I return home and it was time for business all over again. I put together my own Christmas hair and fashion show. I always give away toys to kids and have a skit with meaning and inspiration for my audience. I had a $250 best dressed contest. I also had a dance group called the off the chain dancers. There were praise dancers, singing. It was a huge success. The salon was booming then here comes a huge problem, the owner of the plaza sold it to some man in another state. He wanted me to buy my space and he said the price would be $220.000. He was crazy 960 sq. Ft, I didn't even own my own house! So, we had to find somewhere else to go after 8 yrs there. A friend of mine found a spot back in the neighborhood and I went to see it and I liked it. Me, my daughter and another stylist moved in and I hooked it up real nice. The rent was much cheaper. My oldest daughter and her husband and family found a home in Port St Lucie Fl and while they were waiting on the closing, my younger daughter and her husband moved there before them and rented a house. I was all alone in West Palm. Where I lived was on a main road and I used to walk my dog at least 3 miles for me to exercise. All I ever wanted to do was to grow old gracefully and the weight came off more and everything was in place and my health was great plus I was eating right. I became too sexy for the men, I guess. I used to come home and there were phone numbers in my door and sometimes hall mark cards, men inviting me to dinner and a walk on the beach. I was very single and one day my daughter and I went to Red Lobster for lunch and in walked this young man with his mother, my daughter knew him from the Glades and his sisters. Our eyes locked in on each other, he started talking to my daughter and watching me at the same time. She was asking him how everyone was doing. I went to the restroom while they continued to talk. When I returned my daughter said, "ma he wants to know if he could have your number." I said, "yes!!" from there he called me that evening and asked if he could come see me the next day and every other day after that for about 7 months. It was so intense, the laughter the sex, even the conversation. He made me a music C D that was beautiful, every song was pertaining to something that had to do with our relationship. He would always play it when we contact each other, body contact. Sometimes we would just hold each other, laugh and talk. He was younger than me, but he was very intelligent. He was very funny, always helping the community and so much more. We started growing apart because of the distance and both of our jobs, but we remain friends and every now and then he would call or text. Then eventually that faded away also, I just stop answering my phone because something would always come up either for him or me. I started being afraid of living there alone once again. Some men had been watching and knowing that no man lived with me. Soon the apartment complex started renting out to drug dealers. I had to park my car in the back of the complex and I lived on the front, so I had to walk through the whole complex to get home. I hated it because young guys were hanging out everywhere. I was walking through one evening and this guy said, "hey miss!!" Tell your ole man all these young nigga's watching you.

    I continued to walk with my head straight. He said, "hey you hear me! Tell your ole man all these young nigga's watching you." I looked back and said, "I guess it's okay to look as long as you don't touch me!!" Then he said, "oh yea that's right." With a little grin. I was really scared, even though I had a dog and he would bite someone in a minute, but he was so small.

Sometimes my daughter would send her husband there just so they would see a man coming in and out of my house. I met a good friend at one of the church programs, he is 6'6, slim but tall.

He would come by a lot just to protect me and make sure I was okay. I felt much better, but he couldn't stay because he had his own family. I met another woman in the complex who was white but was with a black man, we became best friends, we made ourselves sisters. We used to smoke together, and I would sit on her porch with her because he didn't want her out of his eyesight. I had to walk by her apartment to get to mine. I would walk by and call her name and asked her if she could come out and play. We would just laugh. I remember one evening we were sitting on her porch laughing and talking and her man was in the house watching television, she open the door and saw me on her big screen t v. he was standing to the door trying to listen to us talk. He bumped his head on the wall trying to run. He had put cameras up which she knew, but he told her it was for when they were inside the house or asleep, when all the time he wanted to watch us. "That was so funny." I would try my best to make her laugh because she had a lot of issues from her past like I did. He didn't like me hanging around that much, but she would insist on us being sisters. I even taught her how to get some booty by exercising. She kept complaining about he liked booty and she didn't have any. The last time I saw her, she had gained quite a bit. I can truly say I haven't seen her in a while, but I really miss her and love her like a sister. We try to stay in touch by phone, but that is not often now. 4yrs I lived there then I told my daughter that I was going to either gain my weight back or move. The men were too much for me to handle. It was not flattering it was scary. I was in my late 40's. And sometimes I would come home, and the police would have the whole area blocked off because of drugs or shooting. "It was time to go!" I did both, gain weight and moved. I moved in a townhouse and the lady would rather me not have a dog. I had to give my dog up after 2 ½ yrs. That was another sad day for both of us. When I walked out of my youngest daughter house where I left him for her husband to give him to a lady who wanted him, he started hollowing like a cry, I ran back in and gave him a big hug. I went back towards the door and started again as if he knew this was his last time seeing me. I cried and cried driving down the highway. Then my vision got blurred and I had to stop, but in my heart, I was still crying. I lived in my place with my oldest granddaughter. I was going to church every Sunday wanting and trying to change my life for the better. I decided to stop smoking marijuana and I had stop going out long before now.

The father kept telling me he was going to buy me a truck because I had a five speed kia that was killing my knees. While he was gone, I tried to buy me an automatic car, so I went to a dealership, first a person that was new there came to assist me. Then someone that had sold my daughter a car prior came and took over. Instead of a car he took me to see a new truck, and he said, "if you want it, I will put you in it." I was like, "how?" I know my credit wasn't that good. Then he said, "let me handle this." I said, "okay." He sent the paperwork through and he said, "it's yours." I told him the payment was too high, and he said, "I will pay 200 for you each month until I can get you refinanced." I said, "why would you do this for me? You don't even know me, he said, "because I know your daughter and these white folks think that black folks are not suppose ride like this." I said, "how do I know each month you will keep your word." He said, "my word is my bond." So, I fell for it, a new truck! It wasn't long before he started hitting on me when I went to pick up the money he promised to pay. I told him I had no interest in him.

After about 6 payments I almost had to fight him for the 200. Then I went there and the whole place was out of business. Now the finance company is riding me, threaten me because at the same time this thing came that was called RECESSION!! The only way I made money is if I had customers to walk in the salon. Everyone was having a hard time. I had to give the truck back, but I got me another car from a buy here pay here first. I prayed and prayed I would not lose the salon. The owner came and said to me, I know it is very slow so pay me what you can on the rent. "That was nobody but God." It got bad I almost lost that car, but I continued to pray and trust God words. One Sunday morning I was looking at TD Jakes and decided to cook me and my granddaughter some breakfast. I put grease in the frying pan, and it started a fire in the pan.

I picked up the pan and the flames felt like it went over my entire body while I was trying to run out the front door. "I just knew I was burned from my head to my stomach." I turned around and run back to the kitchen and the flames got taller and the smoke was filling up the house. I run up the stairs and scream for my granddaughter to wake up! I told her the house was on fire. She ran down stairs and the flames were all over the kitchen cabinets. I just fell back on the stairs and cried. She said, "grandma I got it!" She said, "open the sliding glass door." I screamed, "I tried, it wouldn't open!" She went right to the door and it opened. I grabbed the pan and threw it on the patio. I know that whole townhouse should have been burned down to the ground. The only thing happen is that a knob on the stove burned and the place was full of black smoke upstairs and downstairs, all the furniture. There was not one burn on those cabinets.

"God showed up once again." The smoke alarm was so loud, no one came but God. We got dressed and we went to church anyway, that was my testimony for that day. We both were crying as I was talking, and we wiped our nose, it was full of black smoke. My granddaughter was trying to find a job in West Palm Beach, she couldn't find one. She visited her mom and got a job in Port St Lucie Fl, she moved with her mom and I was left alone again. I had a tread mill that I kept behind the front door. Upstairs in my bedroom I had a chair behind the door, and a knife under my pillow with the bible. I started visiting my daughter in Port St Lucie and it was a house for rent right next door to her. The next visit the owner was there cutting the grass, I asked if I could look inside the house. He said, "sure," "it was beautiful." I asked about the rent payment and what did it take to get in it. I was like wow!!!" Large three bedroom, three bath home with screened in patio." Huge bathroom with everything I dreamed of having. It was cheaper than the townhouse I was living in. I couldn't believe it. I called the father and told him I needed help to get in it. He changed no words, he was upset that I had to give up my dog. But he didn't mind helping me and wanted me to be happy. Soon he came back to Fla and he and his mom and sister came to see the house and his mom decided she wanted to find her a house here too. They fell in love with my house. I hadn't even unpacked my boxes and she wanted me to ride around with her to find her a house. We finally found one for her and she moved in right away just like I did. I was still very closed to the young niece, she began going to church with us and her mom was going every now and then. Some of them didn't like that because of the different religion. I told them that I heard it was hard to find a job here, but they moved anyway. Soon I hear about my younger daughter spending a lot of time with his family. "All hell broke loose!" So much, she said, they said stuff. His mother came to my house to talk to me and I would never disrespect anyone mother. We had a serious conversation and she assured me that everything was good, but she was angry with her granddaughter because she knew that's where I was getting my information. Of course, everyone denied their part in the matter. "Life goes on." He came to my house when he came down and of course she told him whatever my daughter supposedly said, he talked to me about some of it. But he said some things that was said he would keep it to himself. I was fine with that because in my lifetime I have been through worse. He left and the biggest fight of their lives, his son lost. We talked on the phone and I told him remember I told you that you should have never said that about Jesus. He told me that I was a witch. I said, "I'm not a witch!! I just know better." He said, "I mean a good one," he said, "you remind me of those old black slaves that say things to become true." "I just knew where my help really come from." He asked me about moving to New York and working there as a hairstylist. I told him it was too far from my family and I hate cold weather. "So, we remain friends." Soon his family moved and left the state of Fl. The niece got married to her boyfriend and remained in West Palm Bch. I heard that I was blamed for them moving here and there were no jobs here. Really! all I did was showed them my house. Her and her grandmother still are not as close as they should be. But the love for her will always be with my family and her. We always stay in touch with each other and always will. She will soon be 26, that's 13 years of love. I finally paid off my car and that was one of the happiest days of my life. "Here it is almost 19 yrs later who sent me their number?" The sheriff once again he made my heart jump. I was still doing the family hair after all these years also. I called him as soon as I got the number and I told him we are almost too old now. I told him I couldn't believe he finally want a date. "When really it was me in the past who were running." Now I find out that all alone he had been living with someone, but I couldn't tell because during the years of doing his family hair there use to be different women coming in my salon talking to his mom about him. Some things were funny, some were bad that they were saying about him. "I used to say in my mind, just give him to me! Because their bad was wanting me to spend more time with him." I let him know that I wanted to see him but only when he got free. He said, "why don't we just try and see what happens." At the time my heart didn't care because I had waited so long to be with him. But my head was saying don't get in the middle of that. He asked if he could come to my house so we could talk. Of course, I said, "yes." He came that evening and I was so nervous like a young school girl. We sat down and had a good conversation, that night was called breaking the ice. When he got ready to leave, I had to tip toe to kiss him. OMG!!! He could kiss I mean that old school kissing. I told him about how I used to watch him years ago outside my apartment and he asked me why I didn't say anything. I told him I wasn't going to let them sisters jump me. He said, "we waste a lot of years." I said, "look at us now, we were two totally different people back then but now we are very mature." He started coming more often and I would cook for him and sometimes he would wash the dishes for me. The very first time we made love he would take me by the hand, we would kiss all the way to the bed. My inside was like a burning fire that only he could put out. And he surely was worth the wait. His 6'2 body and my 5'3 body fit like a hand inside a glove. We were going strong and feelings were rushing in from every angle. One day I was working, I got a text from him and it said, "I have a secret and it's only for you." He said, "I am in love with you." My heart started pounding. "I was blushing all day." I didn't respond at the time, but I loved him too, but wasn't ready to let him know. When and if I told him, it would be face to face. "I was happy he told me." He was the perfect gentlemen, I remember sometimes I could just think I needed something, he would already be coming through the doors of my salon or knocking on my door at home. My birthday came and he showed up with this little bag that had a great big gift in it. "I was so happy I could just turn a flip." After a few months I ended the relationship because I didn't like being a third wheel anymore. I told him if he ever decided to leave and I was single, then we could continue this love affair. I knew I had to stick to what I wanted from him. "Trust me it wasn't something easy for me to do."

Chapter 12

NOBODY BUT GOD

Here comes the landlord to my house telling me that his house is going into foreclosure, so I had to move in with my daughter and her husband and grandchildren. "Good I only had to move next door." I had so much stuff!!!! I had to get a storage. I had gained so much weight worrying about money and all the bills coming every month. Bills do not care about what you're going through, they just want to be paid. Things were so bad, it had been a long time since I felt helpless or dead broke. It's like every time we made money it belong to someone else. We were driving 100 miles to work and back home. I laid in bed one night and I asked God to take the breath out of my body. I asked him if he would allow me to drive to West Palm by myself and flip the car and I die instantly. "I don't know why, it's not like I had any life insurance to be buried with." "I thought my family would be better off without me." I have always tried to be there for my family and now I was mentally lost. "The devil had just taken my mind." "I knew what God could do, he had already done so much already. I felt as though God was mad with me for the sin I had committed once again." That's another reason I had to end it because when you're sitting in church and you hear what he wants from you and the do's and don'ts you start feeling guilty. The next morning, I went into my daughter room and I asked her to play this gospel song call SPEAK LIFE. I told her what the devil made me asked God to do, only that's not what God does, he restore life. She gladly put the song on, and I cried, she wrapped me in her arms and cried with me. We were there crying for almost an hour. She told me that those were much needed tears that she needed to release. She prayed for me and told me that she loved me, and we were going to be okay. Then we looked at each other and laughed. I had gained so much weight, normally when I am stressed, I would go shopping, so I substitute it with food because I had no money to shop with. I joined the gym but after I really couldn't spend that much time in there within a year I decided to stop going and just walk in the park where they had an exercise trail. "It wasn't that much money but that was money I could pay another bill with. My daughter came and told me that their house was in jeopardy of going into foreclosure. We continued to try and help each other but this was the first time ever that I couldn't do too much to help and neither could she. Her husband lost his job and he was trying to find another job everywhere. I was at work and the sheriff came by and asked if he could take me to lunch so we could talk. I finished what I was doing, and I took him to a place that my granddaughter had taken me to before. We looked at each other and smile, then he told me that he had made up his mind to leave home and get his own place. "I felt as though he was just telling me what he thought I wanted to hear." He said, "This would be the first time I ever lived alone." "I wanted to jump for joy, but I stayed cool." I just said, "Whatever you decide just make sure that's what you want to do." He said, "I thought about it for a long time and I am sure." He said he only told one person besides me but not her yet. At the time his sister's wedding was coming up and I had her hair hooked. She was beautiful and when he walked in that church with his tux on, I wanted to run up there and just wrap my arms around him. I had to remember that I was in church and so was she. At the reception as I walked up to the table where the bride and groom were sitting, I looked over at him and he winked his eye at me. My smile was as big as the building and that was a huge building. After I finished eating, I needed a toothpick, so I remembered I had some in the truck. I told my daughter that I will be right back. When I looked in the back of the place, there stood him and her. I continued to walk, and as I was passing by, she looked at me and said, "Heyyyy girrrrl!!!!" She reached out to hug me. I gently hugged her back but with a lot of guilt, and she wanted to talk but I was trying to walk and talk real fast at the same time. I was so happy that I could come back in the place in another door. I went back to my table. Later I looked back there, and she was gone. He was standing back there with some of his friends. He beckoned for me to come to him. When I returned he introduced me to his friends, I felt so honored for him to even want me to me his friends. I heard one of them tell him that I was pretty. Then he told me how beautiful I looked and then I complemented him. I continued to fight off the temptation until he left. I think it took him about 4 months to move out. Once he settled in his own place, he called me and gave me directions to get there. I was surprised he really left. I packed my bags and jumped in my car and off I went. When I got there, it was beautiful for a man to have hooked it up. He prepared dinner for us and he could cook. YES!! I went and took my shower again, because I had taken one before I left home but there's nothing wrong with a little extra cleansing. And you know the rest! We were very hungry for each other. I was going to see him as much as I could because he really became a workaholic. Then it became once a month or sometimes two months before I could see him, from both of us working. Only he was doing doubles and seems like to me triples. We kept the phone communication opened. A couple of years later, he called me and told me he had brought a house. I offered to help him, and he did except my offer. He called me and told me that he was ready to move, and I drove down and helped him pack some boxes. We used my car and his truck. He did all the heavy lifting that he could until his brothers could help him. Once everything got moved, I decorated his kitchen and the master bathroom. The formal living room was decorated by the both of us. We went to different stores to purchase items to enhance what he already had. It all came together beautifully. After that we Christen the house, you know what I mean… In 2010 my second oldest granddaughter came and told us that she had joined the Army!! What more could have happened? We tried to talk her out of it, but she had already taken her test with her best friend, and they were on their way. They sent her to Oklahoma for basic training. She used to call home angry sometimes and sometimes crying. All I could say was you went behind our backs and joined, so baby just hold on because this too shall pass! She made it and we scraped up all the money we had and all of us went to Oklahoma to her graduation. As soon as I saw her, I cried like a baby, to see my baby in that Army uniform. I had nephews in the Navy and Army, but this was my daughter's child. My granddaughter!! The following year, of all days on April fool day, I decided to leave the salon early because I wanted to walk, because I would normally walk that morning. But I rushed to get there before it got too dark. I went alone and I went around once. I decided to go around the trail again. As I was walking fast, a couple was coming toward me, so I decided to move over to give them room. When I first went around, I met them, and I spoke, but neither of them said anything. So, when I moved over the sidewalk was uneven and I tripped and fell forward. The man who didn't speak ran towards me and asked me was I okay? I told him, I think so. Then he said, "But you're bleeding." I looked down and my right knee and right arm was bleeding. I tried to keep walking, but my knee and my back started hurting and the bugs were flying everywhere. So, I turned around and went back to my car and called my daughter. I told her, "Girl your mama done fell in the park!!" She said, "Naw ma, that's why I never wanted you out there by yourself." I heard her husband say you know it is April fool day. I said, "This is not an April fool joke, I fell for real!!!" She asked me, where was I. I told her I was going to try to make it home. We got home and she put meds on my wounds and the next day I went to work. While I was working my leg, hip, and back started hurting bad. I had to ask my daughter if she could finish for me. The next week Monday my daughter and her husband left home to take my other grandsons to Georgia to spend the summer with their mom. I was supposed to go but couldn't. When they got back with the car I went to the hospital because I could feel and hear my bone pop in my knee. When I got there, they took x-rays of my knee and I came home with a mobilizer and crutches. I was told I needed an MRI taken. The next day I called the office to where I fell and told them they needed to fix the sidewalk and explained what happen. I told them exactly where I fell. They got smart with me and I knew I needed a lawyer. I called this lawyer and they got me in their office right away. I talked to a paralegal of the firm and she wrote down everything and then told me, we don't send people to doctor's but there is this Urgent clinic in Jenson Beach that you could go to. She gave me the address and I went there. The doctor checked my knee and he sent me to have an

MRI done on it. I told him the pain was so bad that something was wrong with my back too. He said the pain was just coming from my knee up to my back. They gave me an ice pack treatment and stimulation on my back. I was going there at least twice a week. I kept complaining about my back and he continued to say it was from my knee. They called in a knee specialist and he did an x-ray in the office and he told me that unfortunately when I fell, I really messed myself up and he didn't advise surgery because he was afraid that it would be worse. He also said that I would never be able to wear high heels anymore. I sat there and I cried like a baby. I couldn't imagine wearing flats or low heel for the rest of my life. He said he would do the surgery if I really wanted him to. I told him I didn't want the surgery and you said you was afraid it would be worst!!! So, he gave me a shot of cortizone in my knee and told me to continue therapy. By the time I got home my whole leg was swollen. I was afraid so I called the doctor and he told me to elevate my leg and put an ice pack on it. He said if it turned red to go straight to the hospital. I continued therapy for my knee and my back with a new doctor, but in the same office. He was a dream come true. He would listen to my pain and let me cry on his shoulder. He worked under my first doctor. The pain in my back continued to get worse, so I called the attorney office and told them something is wrong with my back and the doctors keep telling me that it's from my knee. She told me to call the head doctor, who I was seeing when I first came in wife, and she would tell me who I needed to see. She did. The office kept trying to get me an appointment with him, but they were having no luck getting me in right away. 5 months later they finally got me I, and he still didn't show up. His assistance came. She checked my knee and determined that it was swollen. She looked at my doctor and said, "Have you thought that it maybe her back causing so much pain to her knee?" And he said, "Wow!!! I forgot that." She sent me to have an MRI on my back and asked me to get the disc. I carried that disc in my purse for 4 months, because they kept saying he's in surgery or he is booked up. Finally, I got an appointment. Me and two of my stepsisters went to my appointment. When we went in the office, his assistance showed me the MRI and she called the surgeon in to explain to me what was happening with my back. When he walked in, he was so young and handsome. I asked him did he start school when he was 10? He just laughed at me. The doctor said that I needed surgery and I had a disc that was lying on my left and right nerve on my right side, and that the disc was leaking. He said, "I can do any kind of surgery you need." He said he could do my surgery with his eyes closed. And if he needed surgery, he wished he could do his own. My imagination soared!!! My stepsisters and I were shocked that he said all of that. I told him I didn't want any kind of surgery on my back, if I didn't need it.

But if he could do it with his eyes closed, I felt as if he was the best since sliced bread. He gave me a month to think about it. During this same time, I am coughing and choking every night. Most of the time I coughed and choked so much until I vomit. It was just white foam that I was vomiting. I thought I was dying. I went to the emergency room for that and they gave me medicine for bronchitis. I continued for six months with this choking until they gave me some pain medication for my back, and it stopped. I was so confused because I heard so many horrible stories. I would cry and pray for an answer from God. The attorney was on my case about having the surgery. He was very upset with me because I was taking my time about it. I told him that I was not having surgery for money. He said it looks like you need infusion done. I was like, "Oh no I don't!!!!" I had already read about those Infusions! The doctor told me that he would go in on my right side and move the disc off my nerve and stop the leakage. He said, "I'm no doctor, but you might as well get the infusion now because you're going to need it anyway." I said, "No!!!" Then he said, "Well, just have the surgery and we will go from there." I was ok with that because I was worried about the leaking. I thought maybe that's why I was coughing and choking. I got an apartment in West Palm Beach with a stepsister I had not seen in maybe 10 yrs. She said she would stay with me and make sure I was taken care of, because my daughter had to drive back and forth to work, and my doctor's main office was there. My youngest daughter lived in Georgia. I had no clue how I was going to pay my part of the bills, but I had enough to move in. I had to move out of the salon because I could no longer tolerate the pain. On May 2012, I went into surgery. It was outpatient surgery. When I got home, I was still drowsy and in so much pain. The next day I notice that I had this huge bandage on the left side of my back. I told my daughters and my sisters that he told me that he was going in on my right side. I kept asking, "Why did he go on my left side!!" I guess he did do it with his eyes closed. I wouldn't recommend him doing his own surgery either!!!! I couldn't walk or bathe myself for a long time. My sisters did it for me. When I went to my first appointment, I didn't see the surgeon. I saw his assistance. During this time my daughter called me to tell me that my oldest granddaughter was pregnant. I was so happy to hear that. Finally, some good news. I asked the doctor's assistance, why did he go in on my left side when he said he was going in on my right side. She told me it didn't make a difference. He could still do what he needed to do.

I'm no doctor but that sounded strange to me. If it was her, would she have said that? I told her I was having bad headaches, and she sent me to have an MRI on my neck. I left her office and went straight there to have the test on my neck. When I finished, I went and dropped it back off to the doctor's office so the surgeon or his assistance could look at it and see what was going on. I never got a call back on my neck. She had already told me not to sit or stand no longer than 20 minutes, and no lifting. I continued to go downhill. I was in the worst pain ever. The assistant referred me to see a therapist because she thought I was in a state of depression and having anxiety attacks. Ah yeah!! You think!!! That night my whole right leg was swollen, and I was in so much pain. The pain pills wouldn't even stop it. I tried to see the surgeon, but I could never see him. I did not sleep for a whole week because the pain was so severe. Finally, they gave me an appointment to see him, and before I could see him the office called me and told me that he had left the office for good. I asked, "Where did he go?" They said that they didn't know. They told me that they had another doctor in his place. I called the attorney and they told me to go to a doctor for my knee. They thought that was why my leg was swollen. I went to see the new surgeon for my back first, and he sent me to have another MRI with dye injected in it, so he could see why I was in so much pain. I took that the same day and they gave me the films to take to him. Then, I got a phone call from my daughter telling me that my second oldest granddaughter that's in the Army, was pregnant too. I thought she was kidding. Two babies added to our family in one year. The next day I went to another doctor for my knee and they took x-rays of my back and knee. The doctor came in and told me that the pain was from my back and not my knee. He told me that he was not going to touch me, because all the other doctors had done enough damage to me and he wasn't going to contribute to this mess!! I looked at him like he was crazy. He said, "I will call your attorney and tell them to make sure you have medical for the rest of your life because you're going to need it!!!!!" Then he put me out of his office. I felt like he needed anger management. He made me feel like I had done something wrong. Two days later my brother and I went back to the surgeon, and he looked at the MRI and came and sat in the chair and explained to my brother and I that I had a disc leaking gel on my right side, and the disc was on my left and right nerve, running down my right leg. He said that it was pressing more now than the first MRI that I had taken for the first surgeon. He said that I needed surgery right away. I then told him that I had just had surgery supposedly for the same thing he was telling me. I said but he went in on my left side instead of my right. He asked if he could look at it. I said, "Sure." He said, "Well I'm going in on your right side!!" I said to him, "I don't even know who to trust and I trusted him, I'm going to have to think about this and talk to my family." He gave me a prescription to stop the pain, gave me an appointment to come back in a couple of days. "My family was in an uproar." It had only been almost a month since I had the last surgery. My youngest daughter came from Georgia and my oldest daughter and her husband and the stepsister I was living with, we all went to see the doctor, when I was called in the back, I ask the nurse if my family could back to talk to the surgeon and she said, "Yes all of them could come." We went in the examination room and waited and waited and waited. The doctor kept walking by the room and would never come in. An hour later he sent in a doctor's assistance to talk to us. He was trying to explain and one at a time my family member would ask him why the doctor won't come in and talk to us, he said he didn't know he just sent him in to talk to me. My family and I were very upset, why would a doctor do that? "I was so depressed, didn't know what to do or think." Then the administrator walked in and asked if she could help and I explained what was said to me about the surgery and my family and I wanted to know why in just almost a month I already need another operation. She got my records and told me that the first surgeon owed it to me for another visit after surgery. I told her he wouldn't see me and left before I could see him for my appointment. Now you all have this new surgeon who won't even come in and tell us what is going on. She said well he ask me to tell you that you can call him for a conference call, he will talk to your family then. I told her, "No thank you!" You're going to call me on the phone and then cut me open and I don't know you and you don't know me. "I don't think so!" I went and request my medical records from their office. When my oldest daughter and I went through the medical records we notice that I had thyroid problems and a goiter in my neck. I said, "WOW!" She didn't even call me to let me know any of this! I call the attorney to try and find another surgeon. They said they would try to find someone else. My brother told me about a surgeon who operated on his mother-in-law, so I called the office and explained to his assistance what happen. And she told me she had to talk to the doctor, I gave the attorney his name and they reached out to him also, concerning my situation. They didn't think that he would see me because they said he didn't like working behind other doctors. Later that day the doctor assistance called me and told me that he would see me. "I was so happy!!" I went to see a counselor at the behavior center and from there I talked to a psychiatrist who said I really need therapy. The psychiatrist put me on Zoloft for depression and anxiety. I got so depress until one of my grandsons made me a gospel c d for me to listen to. One of my pain medications had me hallucinating, so I decided to stop taking them. I cried out to God and asked him to please help me and not let me die into the hands of the enemy. I promised him whatever he needed me to do I would do it for the rest of my life. My stepsister left me alone to go visit her son in another part of Fl and I was alone. All I remember is seeing sun up and sun down. The sheriff continued to call me, but I would not answer because I hated myself. "How could you love someone else when you don't even love yourself?" I had already been in the bed for 4 months before my appointment to see this new surgeon. At one point I thought I would lose my mind, I just could not walk, and I surely couldn't sit for a long period of time. My oldest daughter and her husband would come by to check on me sometimes and surround me and pray for me. I could not believe that not one church member come by to pray for me or call to see how I was doing, even the pastor and she got her hair done every week by my daughter. I had been a member there for at least 8 years. "I had to really do some praying for myself." I went in to see the new surgeon and I took my MRI and he looked at them and we had a consultation. I told him the first surgeon and the attorney was trying to talk me into having infusion, and he said, "I'm glad you had sense enough not to." I said, "he told me it would take at least a year to heal." He said, "just like I said I'm glad you didn't and especially not by these MRI's." He told me he would have to do a Discogram to see where the pain was coming from. Then he said, "I am going in on your right side." He did it as outpatient surgery I was right back under anesthesia. "I could feel the pain when he shot the dye into my back." I went home, in the bed again. It was soon time for my oldest granddaughter to have her baby, so she came and stayed with me until she went in labor. I was in so much pain, but I had to be there to see my first great granddaughter come into this world. I went in the next week and the surgeon told me that I needed to have surgery to stop the leakage from my disc and burn the disc off my nerves on my right side. He gave me pain medication and we schedule my surgery for the next month in his office. I heard that he was the best, so I was just ready to get on with my life. I spent 3 years predominantly in bed. "I couldn't understand why I was being punished so much in this lifetime." My stepsister returned and she was taking good care of me for a while. I then told her I had to have another surgery and before I could have it the next month she left for another stay with her son. Only this time she did not come back, she would not answer any of my phone calls and it was time to pay rent. I text her and she would not respond back. "As if I wasn't already depressed enough!" I sent my daughter by the rent office to let them know what she had done, and they tried to reach her to see what her plans were. She would not talk to anyone but my brother. I was just getting ready to pay the rent and just ask for my money when she return, my brother told me the way she was talking he didn't think that she was coming back. He said, "She told him not to tell me that he had talk to her," "I couldn't understand unless it was too much to take care of me." "I would have understood that." I had to move out of my apartment before my surgery only I couldn't do much of nothing. I was so hurt that she just couldn't tell me, I looked around at all of my furniture and how beautiful the place was, and I just screamed and cried. "I kept asking why!" My daughter just held me in her arms and said, "Mama you just got to do what you got to do." She said, "I am here for you always and her and her husband and my grandchildren packed my things and I moved in Port St Lucie Fl once again with them." The following month I had my surgery and I had to wear a back brace for a few months until the surgeon told me to try and wean myself away from it. During my sickness my family took real good care of me. Especially my son-in-law who made sure I continue to have something to eat and my daughter who took me to every appointment and continued to come in my room and pray with me when I couldn't go to church or pray for myself. The attorney's and doctors screwed me out of ever trusting in them again. I never got compensated for my back because the therapist lied and said he worked on my knee and my arm instead of my back. "They were all working against me." My attorney got suspended by the bar and that let me know that they were doing some dirty stuff even with me. I ended up with some people I had never talked to that were helping her threaten me. The attorney that worked with their office on my case ended up committing suicide a month later. The way I found out is from another attorney I went to see about malpractice on the first surgeon. She said, "Even though you have evidence showing that he went on the wrong side of your back, you didn't go into a coma or die from it." She said, "I am sorry that's the Fl Law." "I thought to myself hell I am glad I didn't go through any of that!" "Everything that could go wrong did once again." "I thank God for Jesus because if it had not been for prayer, I don't know where I would be now." "I had to get an attitude that's says, it is what it is!" I continue to grab a whole of my life and continued therapy and going to see my psychiatrist and tried to take one day at a time. During this time, I was getting tested for a colonoscopy and one where the doctor went down my throat into my stomach at the same time, when the test results came back, he said, "Your colonoscopy test was good, but I am concerned about the bacteria I found in your stomach." He said he had to put me on medication for a month because it was the kind that could turn into stomach cancer. "Praying time again," My grandchildren and my daughter and her husband band a circle and we prayed. That's something we do all the time, most of the times just because how good God is. A month later I had to take some stool to the lab to be tested to see if the bacteria was gone. "Hallelujah!!! It was gone!" Then one day I was on this dating site because I had nothing else better to do, and this man wanted to be my friend and he lived here where I lived only he thought I lived in West Palm Bch Fl, he sent me his phone number and I called him, we were on the phone for an hour laughing and talking. We continue to talk for 3 months and I invited him to come see me at the house. He walked in the house and I could tell that he was nervous. My whole family was at home. He looked at me and he told me I was even prettier in person. I just sat there and blush. He was 6'5 and dark skinned and very handsome. I introduce him to my family and before he left, he said, "I have something for you." He walked to his truck and came back with a rose. My daughter teased him saying, "You wanted to make sure she was worth that rose first huh?" He just laughed and so did I. We continued to talk on the phone and enjoyed doing so, I explained everything that was going on with me about the surgeries and he told me he just wanted me to get well. I started getting up more trying to regain my strength so I could date this man. But it was a very slow healing. I tried to walk to the corner when my granddaughter came home from the Army to have her baby. "Their babies were 2 months apart." "Her labor almost sent me back to surgery! She was in labor for 16 hours." When she had her daughter, she is my second great granddaughter, how amazing is that. Then a few months later my oldest grandson came and told me that his girlfriend was pregnant. "These are all 3 of my oldest daughter children, now time for her to be a grandma." I became NANA. I finally got invited out to dinner by my new friend, I dressed nice and with everything in me I tried to pretend that I wasn't in any pain, but it was obvious. "He was a true gentleman he opened the car door for me, he even carried my purse for me!" I enjoyed the dinner and we laughed and talked. He drove me home, walked me to the door and said goodnight. The next week he invited me to come over and stay all night. "When I got there his house was looking like something that I had decorated, it was beautiful inside." He told me to make myself at home. I was a little nervous, but I am the type of woman to never let them see me sweat. He made us dinner, he cooked us a nice big steak on his grill and made a salad and veggie's. "It was excellent." We sat down and talk and every now and then when I pass by him, I could see his eyes touching my booty. I took a nice hot shower and he turned his television on in his bedroom where his nice big king size bed is. He turned the covers back as we lay across the bed watching a movie, we held each other and I think we both was scared to death but, he was still a Gentlemen. He told me he needed to finish some work in his home office. The next morning, I wondered where he was, he was in the kitchen cooking me breakfast. I asked him what happen to him last night and he said, "woman I walked back in here and you were snoring so loud and whistling with it!" I started laughing saying, "you're lying." He laughed and said, "I went back to work because I knew I wasn't going to rest anyway." We both just laugh, then he said, "After I finish work, I just went in the other bedroom." We sat around that day on his patio and talk more and we listen to music and I did get a little dance out of him. That evening he made me dinner again and took me home. He love to cook too, I tried to help but he insist on doing it all by himself. That was one of the best dates I ever been on to a man house. "The only date I ever been on and no pressure to have sex." We stayed in touch by phone and he love that I make him laugh. He is a very educated man, so some of my ebonics, I had to break it down so he could understand, and it was funny to him. "I thought about this man is single he has never been married and has no children, he is his mom only child." "He lived alone and has no drama in his life why would he want to continue seeing me." "I have a big family and had all these different operations on my back and living with my daughter and her husband, can't work anymore." So, I decided to text him and explain to him how sorry I was inviting him in my life with my drama." "I didn't know it was around his deceased father birthday." He was so upset with me he didn't want to talk to me anymore. "He waited at least 3 weeks before I heard anything from him." He asked me had he ever complained about anything to me. And I said, "no," he told me it was his dad birthday and I had to add that on top of what he was already feeling. I tried so hard to make him understand that I was sorry for the text, but this man was not hearing me at all. I don't know how true astrology signs are, but Aries are very bull headed. I just said okay and hung up and said, "It is what it is!" I knew I had messed up a good thing, that I may not ever find again, "especially at my age." Time went on and a couple months went by and I didn't hear from him. Soon my phone rang. It was him. We talked. I explained and he explained, and we made an agreement that we would take it slow because he wanted me to concentrate on getting well. My granddaughter started going to a church she was invited to, so I decided that's what I needed to focus on, "God." Love me first then a relationship. During this time, I had a blast from my past call me and wanted to see me, but I was afraid that I would mess things up with the guy who I thought would be a perfect match for me. "It was the sheriff." I continued to go to therapy for my neck and my back. Soon I went to get my thyroid checked and the doctor said that I had nodules on top of the goiter, and I needed a biopsy. "Here comes fear again, the big C (Cancer) that I would have to worry about." The doctor told me that they were the size of a quarter and it could cut it off my esophagus, if it continues to grow. My daughter and her husband had to leave for Maryland when they gave me my appointment for the biopsy, so I called my friend and asked him if he would take me. He said, "Yes." That would be my chance to get him back into my world and show him that I am a caring person, not a selfish person. Like most Aries are, that I know anyway. The day came and I went to have the biopsy. I thought he was going to go with me to hold my hand like my daughter would normally do. He said he had to be on stand-by for his job just in case he got a call. When the doctor looked at my MRI, he said normally I would take you right into surgery to remove your thyroid, but since there was a referral to have a biopsy, I will do that, and we will go from there. I would usually just close my eyes and say to myself mind over matter. Mind over matter, and the pain wouldn't be so bad! But honey, I would not wish this on anyone!! He stuck me at least 6 different times in 6 different places with a needle as big as me!!! One time I remember grabbing his hand and gasping for air. I was so happy when that was over. Now, all I had to do was pray that my test come back negative. He told me to come back in 6 months and he would see if it was still growing. I came out and my friend went looking for his doctor. As we were walking around the building, I put my hand inside his hand and he just looked down at me and smile. You could tell that he got very nervous. I looked up at him and said, "Are you scared!" He said, "No," But he was. Then he tells me he needed to stop by his house to use the bathroom. I laughed to myself and said, "Okay, I'll just stay in the truck." He said you don't have to. I said, "Yes I do." He insisted that I got out once he reached his house. I went in and he did use the bathroom, but once he walked by me, I guess he had to see if my but was real. He rubbed his hand across it. I just laughed at him, and he did ask for some and I said, "No!!" He said in a soft voice, "I'll take you home." I told him on the way home, that at my age and where I was trying to go with God, I was not looking for a quickie. I wanted all of him or nothing. I wanted a God fearing man. Not just any man. "I had enough of them." I told him that I will not miss what I never had. He said, "You're just a teaser, you know you don't want me." I said, "If only you knew how much I want you." Thank God for the great change in me. I feel that he would either like me more or just let go. I was prepared for either. My granddaughter called and told my daughter that she had to go to Afghanistan for a year, and that she had got her papers and they were having a ceremony for them. I knew the ride would kill me, but this is my granddaughter, and her baby was 6 months, and all I could do was to be there for her. My therapist explained to me, how to try to release some of my pain, but it was terrible! 18 hour ride from FL to Texas. We packed up and hit the road when it was time, and the ceremony was nice for them, but I cried like a baby once again. She was leaving us, her baby, and husband. She was holding me asking me not to cry, as if I were leaving. I told her I cannot help it. I said, "You're going into another world and those people don't care or like us." And she said, "Grandma, that's what I am trained for." She had one of the deadliest jobs you could have in the Army. She said, "If you keep crying, you are going to make me cry and I can't." I think it hurt me even more hearing all the children begging their parents not to leave them. It was one of the saddest things I had heard in a long time. She got on that bus that night and I stood in the parking lot and watched them as they drove away, and I cried and cried. I know now that I really needed to get closer and closer to Jesus with all that was going on with us and the world. I was so thankful for skype and us taking turns looking after her baby. I always talked to my friend that used to come by and check on me. The one with the family, just friends. Through all these years, he has always help me stay grounded. I tell him everything, from men to children, grandchildren, siblings and all. He has always been there for me and always will. Well, my granddaughter only had to stay over there for 6 months, but during her stay she had a lot of close calls from bombs and missiles, "I can't even tell you how many times I almost lost my mind." "Sometimes the what If's, scare you more than what could have happened." She made it home 4 days before Christmas. "Yes, we were on the road again." We took my oldest great granddaughter with us so her mom could continue to work. It was freezing going to Texas, and when we arrived. We got there the day before, my son-in-law had made a huge Welcome home sign for her that all the family signed before we left. When we arrived at the building, they were coming in. My son-in-law was trying to hold the sign up, but it was too big. One of the Army people told him to go up the stairs and post in on this big railing, and while he was up there a news reporter came and asked him questions concerning my granddaughter. "I tell you when you get up in age everything goes wrong with your body. All I can say is thank God they made panty liners, because when I saw that young lady walk into that building I started screaming, and piss came down!" LOL. I had to scream softly because I was not about to go to the bathroom." Not now! "I had happy tears and a closer walk with God." After the ceremony the news reporter found her and interviewed her holding her baby. I was standing there with her. Later, that night on the news, they showed my son-in-law and my granddaughter talking, also other soldiers that made it home with her. We stayed in Texas until after Christmas, and by New Year we were back home. Then came time for my appointment with the thyroid surgeon. Prior to my appointment, he had sent me to take another test to see if things were the same or had gotten worse. "Just my luck as usual." He came into the room where my daughter and I were waiting and said to me, "Just as I thought it would be. Things are worst. You need to have your thyroid completely removed and you will have to be on thyroid medication for the rest of your life." He gave me a pamphlet to read about my situation. I looked over at my daughter and I cried because I was tired of being drugged up and on medication. I was tired of surgery after surgery. He told me that once he removed my thyroid, he would have to run more test on it to make sure I was cancer free. I went ahead and made plans to have it done as soon as possible, which was less than a month's time. My youngest daughter and her finance came down for my surgery. I have always tried to be brave for them, but right before the anesthesia I got nervous. Because, this time I had to stay overnight in a hospital to make sure everything goes well before, during and after. My oldest daughter started asking me to stay calm because she did not want me to go into surgery scared and nervous because sometimes it could affect the outcome. She started praying for me and singing my favorite gospel song. Then she told me she was going to get my younger daughter because they only let one in at a time. When she came back, I was still crying but not afraid. My daughter kissed me on my forehead and assured me that everything was going to be alright. Before I knew it, I was in a room with my immediate family there, No siblings. My stepsister, who I hated to refer to her as that, was there with me from the beginning to the end. "Always!" Every time I opened my eyes she was there. My stay went from overnight to five days. She never left my side. They had to make sure I could swallow. I began to have a fever. When I did get a little better to get out of bed, she bathed me and fed me, and she sang to me. Writing this with tears falling from my face, I am so thankful for her. She even brushed my teeth. Now that's my sister!!! I will never forget what she has done for me. I came home with my neck sliced, but he did a great job. She remained with me at home helping my daughter take care of me. My son-in-law made sure that whatever I could eat, I ate. My youngest daughter had to go back to Georgia to work, but I was so happy she came. The next weekend my oldest daughter called me and said my youngest grandson, by my youngest daughter, was at the hospital in a coma!!! I was sitting in the family room trying to get my strength back and I got so worried. She said she had been trying to call his mom, my daughter, but couldn't reach her. I called her phone and she answered it. I told her calmly what I knew and told her she needed to come as soon as possible, to drive safe, and that I loved her. She had just left here during my surgery and had to turn around and come right back here. I had my oldest granddaughter to drive me to the hospital which was about 70 miles from where I lived. When we got to the hospital, his father, stepmother, and siblings on his father side, were already at the hospital. He lived with them. No one warned me before I went in my grandson's room. He was in ICU and I walked in there with my granddaughter. He was hooked to every machine you could possibly be hooked up to. I started crying and screaming, "Lord please. No!!!!" The nurse saw that my neck had strips on it from my surgery and ran and grabbed me before I hit the floor. Her and my granddaughter held me up. They took me out of his room, and I could not believe that my grandchild, was lying there like that. He was only 18 yrs old!!! I couldn't seem to catch my breath and the nurse asked me had I just had surgery. I told her yes. She said you are going to have to calm down or I will wheel you down to the emergency room. I said, crying, "I didn't expect to see him like this."

My granddaughter was crying saying, "Grandma please!!! You're not well, you're sick yourself." I calmed down eventually, and I went back in there and he looked as if he was dying. I couldn't do anything, but hold his hand and cry, and pray. I called my daughter and I warned her of what he was going through. She was crying saying, "Okay ma, I'm on my way." The doctor's kept saying they had him in a medically induce coma, and they didn't know what was wrong with him yet. His dad told me when they were trying to put a tube in him, that the doctor said they made a mistake and punctured a hole in his lungs, but it would heal. My family got there, and we sat and waited on my daughter to get to the hospital from Georgia, before we left. She got there around 1:30am. She went in and my oldest daughter and I went with her. It hurt me so much to see my daughter seeing her child in a battle for his life. We prayed like we could see God standing there saying, "I got him." My oldest daughter and the family that live with us left to get some rest so we could return the next day. They were worried about me, but it was no time for me to think about me. I had to be strong for everyone. I have always been a fighter, and now was the time to fight with all my might. The next day they ran all kind of tests, and still everything was coming up negative. The first 3 days was very critical. They still couldn't figure out what was wrong. It was so many people coming to see and pray for him. I was in so much pain from head to toe. After the fourth day of trying to ride back and forth and sit all day, my body gave out on me. I tried with all my might to get out of bed, but I couldn't. My brain was moving, but my body was still. My sister, that's my sister by my mother, called and asked me how he was doing, and I told her that he was the same. I tried to get out of bed but couldn't, then she said to me, "You've got to make yourself move and get up." I said to her, "Have you forgotten the surgeries I've been through?" Oh, I remembered. She never made it to any of them anyways!! Then she said, "My daughter needs her, I know she is just standing around with her arms folded and don't want to be bothered." Then she said, "You know how she is." I said, "Yes! She is my child. And I took MY child in my arms and held her, and we both cried on each other's shoulder, and she is just fine." I told her she took it better than me. She said, "Oh really?" I said, "Really!!" She said she thought about catching a ride with a friend that lived this way to be with her. But my daughter live in the same town and was coming from Georgia for my surgery and asked her if she wanted to come, but she said she couldn't ride this far. It used to hurt, but know I get where I laugh about it now. (You came down here twice and had to past me to get to where you were going.) BUT YOU LOVE YOUR LITTLE SISTER? Well, Back to my grandson. The next day I went to the hospital and I asked the doctors did they test him to see if he had gotten bitten by something. He asked me, "Did you know something that may have bit him?" I said, "Well, his father house is in the woody area of Loxahatchee." He said, "They are running more test." By the next week Monday, my grandson opened his eyes and was trying to answer us. We all screamed, thank you Jesus!!! He finally made it out of ICU. Then I was told that my daughter, his mom, wanted to take him back to Georgia with her and I just didn't see him going because he was doing better in school and his appearance. He was participating in church. My daughter started telling me that he, suddenly stopped trying to fight to get better. In my mind, I was wondering did she tell him she was taking him back with her. She told me that she had discussed it with him. So, I asked her to ask him what he wanted to do because he would soon be 19 years old, and he should know where he wants to live. She got very upset with me and said, "What's wrong with me wanting to take my child back with me?" I said nothing is wrong with that, but at least find out what he wants to do. She said, "Everybody is always against me!" I said, "No!! I just want him to fight for his life." So, the next day I went to the hospital to see him. I walked up to my daughter and gave her a hug and she told us what room they had moved him to. She went down stairs of the hospital and me, my oldest daughter, and my stepsister went in to visit him, and he looked so good and he had this huge smile on his face. He held my hand and told me that he love me. My eyes filled up with water and I smiled and told him how much I love him. He said, "I know grandma." I told him I think your mom is mad with me, and he said, "She will get over it, and smiled." I felt so much better just to hear him say that. He said, "I told my mom that I'm going back home with my dad." I said, "I just wanted you to know that you had a choice." I had not even talked to him about it. He already knew what the problem was with my daughter and me. My daughter left and went back to Georgia and didn't say good-bye to me. I had to hear from someone else that she was gone. My grandson made it home out of the hospital. He moves around a little slow, but he is still here! I continued my physical therapy for my back and stayed in church as much as possible. I am so happy that my granddaughter went to this church and we all visited it one day. It is almost a year at this new church, and I am loving it. Our Bishop and his wife are the truth and I appreciate being in a real spiritual and loving church. It's on Fire!! My mom/customer always stayed in touch with me to make sure my grandson was doing okay. She kept her promise to me from that day at my mom's funeral, that she would always be here for me and she has done just that. She still calls me to this day. She has gotten sick and older and can't drive as far as she used to. I am glad that I've had her and her family all these years by my side. My youngest daughter just married, and I pray that she lives happily ever after. I continue to talk to my psychiatrist. He said it would be best if I talk to a therapist while I am writing my life story. I have been talking to a therapist. My therapist looks as young as my daughter or younger, but she is smart. She is mostly helping me to understand the things that I've been through and love myself first. I don't think I have ever cried so much, unless I was thanking Jesus for everything, or asking him to help me and this crazy world. "One thing I can say is that I can see things a little clearer now". My goal is to go back to school and further my education and one day teach Cosmetology or open my own school of Cosmetology. I also would love to help different organizations with abused kids or the parents who abuse them. Maybe I can help someone understand that they are "CRYING FOR HELP".

    I thank God that I have two daughters that has always been drug free and has never taken anything that wasn't theirs. I used to always threaten them that if they ever go to jail for stealing. Don't call me because I'm not coming. So, they never went to jail for anything. My eight grandchildren were told the same thing. I have five grandchildren that have graduated, and three of them to prayerfully finish soon. I always teach them to pray about everything and to stay focus. All of them were raised in the church. They are not perfect, but they know right from wrong. They know if they get into any trouble or have a problem to fall on their knees and pray. To my three great granddaughters, D'lasia, Ayzaria, and Baylee, NANA love you all very much and I know that God has you little ones in his hand. I pray all day that God continue to bless me and my family and keep his loving arms around us. I am still living with my oldest daughter and her husband. The best son-in-law you could ever ask for. Not because of anything, just because he is a very humble person and will give you the shirt off his back if you need it. He has always been there for his family and I. My daughter and him has been together for the last 15yrs and still hold hands and kiss each other every day all day in and out of their goings. They are always in Church together and living a Christian life. He and my daughter are true warriors for Christ and that has helped me stay focus on God. I may not be where I want to be in life, but I am surely not where I was. I've learned that when all else fail, TRY JESUS. Truly the best thing to do is try JESUS before all else fails. I continue to be friends with the gentlemen and on Mother's Day the sheriff texted me Happy Mother's Day, then he texted me later and said he really missed me. As far as that goes (Stay Tune). But one thing for sure is that I AM IN LOVE WITH JESUS! I will be 59 soon and don't have any time to waste, so I WILL let go and let God handle my needs and my wants. I am a fighter and will always be a fighter, a different kind of fighting now. FIGHTING FOR MY SALVATION…. And please don't just hear someone. LISTEN TO THEM AND ALWAYS REMEMBER, A WINNER NEVER QUITS AND A QUITTER NEVER WINS!!!

www.ingramcontent.com/pod-product-compliance
Lightning Source LLC
Chambersburg PA
CBHW052048070526
44584CB00017B/2107